T0128393

Fundamental Mind

Fundamental Mind:
The Nyingma View
of the Great Completeness

Mi-pam-gya-tso

With Practical Commentary by
Khetsun Sangpo Rinbochay

Translated and edited by Jeffrey Hopkins

Snow Lion
Boulder

Snow Lion
An imprint of Shambhala Publications, Inc.
4720 Walnut Street
Boulder, Colorado 80301
www.shambhala.com

© 2006 by Khetsun Sangpo Rinbochay and Jeffrey Hopkins

All rights reserved. No part of this book may be reproduced in any
form or by any means, electronic or mechanical, including
photocopying, recording, or by any information storage and retrieval
system, without permission in writing from the publisher.

Printed in the United States of America

∞ This edition is printed on acid-free paper that meets the
American National Standards Institute Z39.48 Standard.
♻ Shambhala Publications makes every effort to print on recycled
paper. For more information please visit www.shambhala.com.
Distributed in the United States by Penguin Random House LLC
and in Canada by Random House of Canada Ltd

Library of Congress Cataloging-in-Publication Data
Mi-pham-rgya-mtsho, 'Jam-mgon 'Ju, 1846–1912.
[Gñug sems 'od gsal gyi don rgyal ba rig 'dzin brgyud pa'i luṅ bźin
brjod pa rdo rje'i sñiṅ po. English]
Fundamental mind: the Nyingma view of the great completeness /
Mi-pam-gya-tso; with practical commentary by Khetsun Sangpo
Rinbochay; translated and edited by Jeffrey Hopkins.
p. cm.
Includes bibliographical references.
ISBN 978-1-55939-250-1 (alk. paper)
1. Rdzogs-chen. 2. Rñiṅ-ma-pa (Sect)—Doctrines. I. Khetsun Sangpo
Rinbochay. II. Hopkins, Jeffrey. III. Title.
BQ7662.4.M529613 2006
294.3'422—dc22
2006004301

Contents

Preface

This is the first translation of *The Meaning of Fundamental Mind, Clear Light, Expressed in Accordance with the Transmission of Conqueror Knowledge-Bearers: Vajra Matrix*[1] by the great Tibetan scholar-yogi Mi-pam-gya-tso[2] (1846-1912) of the Ñying-ma order. This text on the Ñying-ma view of ultimate reality is the first of Mi-pam-gya-tso's trilogy, called Three Cycles on Fundamental Mind, which explains the Great Completeness, the basal nature in which spiritual development is grounded.

Through commenting on the text, Khetsun Sangpo Rinbochay expands on his ground-breaking presentation of the preliminary Tantric practices in *Tantric Practice in Nying-ma*.[3] He begins with a biography of Mi-pam-gya-tso, drawn from and contextualizing his thirteen-volume *Biographical Dictionary of Tibet and Tibetan Buddhism*,[4] and then gives expansive, practical commentary on Mi-pam-gya-tso's introduction, explaining the aim of the book—the differentiation of mistaken mind from fundamental mind. The main theme is primordial enlightenment in the basal clear light, self-arisen pristine wisdom. Then, in four chapters Mi-pam-gya-tso:

- presents basic mind, or vajra matrix, drawing on myriad explanations in Tantras;

- details how fundamental mind is an uncompounded[a] union of luminosity and emptiness;

- refutes Ja-wa Do-ngak's presentation of the Great Completeness as a compounded[b] mind;

---

[a] *'dus ma byas, asaṃskṛta.*

[b] *'dus byas, saṃskṛta.*

- and draws distinctions about the nature and appearance of fundamental mind prior to and after realization.

The emphasis is on introducing fundamental mind in naked experience through a lama's quintessential instructions.

Khetsun Sangpo Rinbochay is a Ñying-ma lama trained in Tibet and capable of transmitting in complete form the special precepts of the Ñying-ma order. A lay priest and renowned yogi-scholar, he was trained in all four lineages of Tibetan Buddhism. He is among the most senior lamas and Great Completeness masters in the Ñying-ma Tibetan Buddhist tradition and is the most eminent Ñying-ma historian alive today.

He was born in 1920 in Yak-de (*g.yag sde*) on the border between the central and western provinces of Tibet and came to India in 1959. He was soon asked by His Holiness the Dalai Lama to represent Dudjom Rinbochay, head of the Ñying-ma school, in Japan, where he spent ten years in this capacity from 1960-1970, teaching in Tokyo and Kyoto Universities and becoming fluent in Japanese.

In 1971 he returned to India and founded a school to educate Tibetan monastics in his tradition, called the Nyingmapa Wishfulfilling Center, in Bouda, Nepal. Over more than thirty years he has accepted numerous invitations to teach in Japanese and U.S. universities and to teach students in retreats in Dordogne, France. He taught at the University of Virginia during the spring semester, 1974, and returned in 1986 to lecture on the Ñying-ma presentation of the two truths and to give a series of lectures and meditations at the Union of the Modern and the Ancient (UMA) in Boonesville, Virginia, on Mi-pam-gyatso's exposition of fundamental mind, on which this book is based.

In Tibet, Khetsun Sangpo Rinbochay received teachings on the Heart Essence of the Great Expanse tradition from the famous Lady Master Jetsun Shuksep Rinbochay (d. 1953) of Shuksep Nunnery, Tibet's main institution for female practitioners of the Great Completeness. His other teachers include Dudjom Rinbochay, Kangyur Rinbochay, and Dilgo Khyentse Rinbochay.

His writings feature an account of his spiritual journey and attainments, titled *Autobiography of Khetsun Sangpo: Memoirs of a Nyingmapa Lama from the Yamdok Area of Tibet*⁵ and a thirteen-volume *Biographical Dictionary of Tibet and Tibetan Buddhism,* an edited compilation of biographies of the masters of all Tibetan Buddhist traditions. His *Tantric Practice in Nyingma* has been used by thousands of students around the world as a guide to the foundational practices.

Jeffrey Hopkins
Emeritus Professor of Tibetan Studies
University of Virginia

Technical Note

In this work, the transliteration of Tibetan follows the system formulated by Turrell Wylie,[6] except that here no letters are capitalized. Also employed here is a system of "essay phonetics,"[7] developed to reflect the pronunciation of words in the central dialect. A macron over a letter indicates that its sound is high in tone.

In the conversion table below, the Wylie transliteration form of Tibetan letters is on the left of each column and the Hopkins "essay phonetics" form on the right.

ka = ḡa	kha = ka	ga = ga	nga = nga or ñga*
ca = j̄	cha = cha	ja = ja	nya = nya or ñya
ta = d̄a	tha = ta	da = da	na = na or n̄a
pa = b̄a	pha = pa	ba = ba	ma = ma or m̄a
tsa = d̄za	tsha = tsa	dza = dza	wa = wa
zha = sha	za = sa	'a = a	ya = ya
ra = ra	la = la	sha = šha	sa = ša
ha = ha	a = a		

* Nasals (*nga, nya, na, ma*) in the root position take on a high tone only when affected by a prefixed or superscribed letter.

At the first occurrence of a number of technical terms, Tibetan equivalents are given, accompanied by the Sanskrit when available. These terms appear together in the Glossary, in English alphabetical order.

The four chapter divisions and titles have been added to the translation to facilitate accessibility.

Biography of Mi-pam-gya-tso

by Khetsun Sangpo Rinbochay

Within adjusting your motivation to seek highest enlightenment for the sake of all sentient beings throughout space, listen to the doctrine today, which is about the life-and-liberation story of the omniscient Mi-pam-jam-ȳang-ñam-gyel-gya-tso.[8] He was born in 1846 in the Kam[9] Province of Tibet in Ya-chu-ding-chung[10] on the banks of the gently flowing [Yalu] River. A very learned uncle on his father's side, Padma-dar-gyay,[11] gave him the name Mi-pam-gya-tso.[12] When he was very young, unlike other children, he was naturally endowed with faith, discipline, renunciation, intelligence, and compassion. In the midst of children he was keen to be helpful and caring, and when children were playing hard and so forth, picking on others, he was protective and encouraged them to be compassionate.

At age six or seven he memorized the root text of Ṅga-ri Paṇ-chen Padma-ŵang-gyel's[13] *Ascertainment of the Three Vows*[14] and so forth, and studied introductory books on white and black astrology. Able to write not only in capital and cursive Tibetan but also in other alphabets, such as Lantsa, at age ten he composed a poem, which when scholars saw it, they were amazed. Thus, in the Kam area, various scholars passed his poem amongst themselves, and even at that age he became famous for his intelligence.

At age twelve he entered ordinary monastic life at Ju-me-hor Ŝang-ñgak-chö-līng[15] Monastery, which is a subsidiary of Se-chen Ḍen-ñyi-dar-gyay-līng Monastery,[16] which itself is a branch monastery of O-gyen Ṃin-dröl-līng Monastery.[17] Everyone called him "the little monk scholar."

At age fifteen, when he was trying to read an ancient

text of white astrology of Svarodaya[18] of the Kālachakra system, he had some difficulty, at which point he made a supplication to Mañjushrī, whereupon he understood all the words and meaning vividly. He realized that Mañjushrī was his particularly special deity and that to repay Mañjushrī's kindness he should gain meditative achievement. So, at Ju-nyung[19] hermitage he practiced Mañjushrī Vādasiṃha[20] for eighteen months and performed the activity rites of sacred Mañjushrī pills, and so forth, for the sake of increasing intelligence. He was successful such that upon the opening of the vast mental expanse all that he had to do with respect to any topic was to receive its reading-transmission,[21] whether it was a book of ritual, philosophy, or debate in the categories of Sūtra, Tantra, or sciences;[22] he would not have to study and be taught as we do. He would know immediately the words and meaning.

When he was seventeen, because of disturbances in Nyak-rong[23] all the nomads moved to Go-lok,[24] due to which he also went there. Around this age he became renowned for his great skill in arithmetic.

At age eighteen, on a pilgrimage to central Tibet with his maternal uncle Gyur-sang,[25] he went to Ganden Monastic University, where he spent about a month engaged in reasoning in the debating courtyard. He traveled extensively in southern Tibet, during which he went to Hlo-drak Kar-chu,[26] almost to the border of Bhutan, where there are many important holy places associated with Padmasambhava. This was also the location of the monk Nam-kay-ñying-b̄o,[27] one of the twenty-five great disciples of Padmasambhava,[28] who became such a great adept that he climbed aboard the rays of the sun traveling from mountain to mountain.

Without intentionally entering into study or meditation, just from the blessings of the place ordinary appearances and conceptions vanished, and Mi-pam-gya-tso experienced various joys of the stage of generation and the stage of completion, in which all appearances dawn as solely the sport of great bliss and emptiness. Since at that time he did not know much about the practice of Mantra, he remarked that it was probably due to the empowering blessings of the area. On the way back north in a vision of pure appearance a book titled *Crystal Mirror of the Great All-Seeing Svarodaya*[29] arrived in his hands, as is described clearly at the end of that text.

Having finished his pilgrimage and returning to Kam, he went to receive teachings from the famous adept Lap-gyap-gön Ŵang-chen-gyay-rap-dor-je,[30] who immediately said, "You are under the care of white Mañjushrī; therefore, you need do only a rite of approximation meditation of white Mañjushrī in accordance with the *ma-ti* system," and he bestowed on him the permission rite to conduct this practice. Both during the initiation and during the ritual activities[31] subsequent to the practice, signs of adepthood manifested, due to which the lotus of his intelligence blossomed.

Then from Ba-drül O-gyen-jik-me-chö-ĝyi-ŵang-bo[42] Mi-pam-gya-tso took teachings on the wisdom chapter of Shāntideva's *Engaging in the Bodhisattva Deeds* over five days, at which point he completely understood the words and the meaning of the text. Having given what was mostly an oral transmission reading, Ba-drül Rin-bo-chay finally said, "I have nothing particular to teach you. You know more about this than I do. I see no point in going on." Later, Mi-pam-gya-tso composed a commentary on the chapter on wisdom,[33] and so forth.

Based on karmic connections over lifetimes, his main teacher for both Sūtra and Mantra was one of the most famous lamas of Kam, named Jam-ȳang-kyen-dzay-wang-bo,[34] who put together a collection of works called the Precious Treasury,[35] which used to be sixty-four volumes and now is around double that number. Though Jam-yang-kyen-dzay-wang-bo's own lineage was Sa-gya, he was skilled in the doctrines of all Tibetan lineages, and he considered Mi-pam-gya-tso to be his unique inner spiritual child. Just as the former lama had done, Jam-yang-kyen-dzay-wang-bo conducted a permission ritual for Mi-pam-gya-tso to practice white Mañjushrī in accordance with the *ma-ti* system, since he saw that Mi-pam was under the care of Mañjushrī.

Jam-yang-kyen-dzay-wang-bo conferred on him many approaches of common and uncommon scriptures; extraordinary texts of Sūtra and Mantra that had been passed to him in direct transmission; and the maturations, releases, supports, quintessential instructions, practical techniques, and experiential instructions of the entire scope of the Word Transmissions, Treasure Transmissions, and Visionary Transmissions of the greatly secret Vajra Vehicle. Having conferred on him the transmissions of all of the three scriptural collections of the discipline, sets of discourses, and manifest knowledge, as well as the four tantras—Action, Performance, Yoga, and Highest Yoga—and their initiations, Jam-yang-kyen-dzay-wang-bo announced, "I have offered to you all of my qualities of education in the manner of pouring from one vessel into another," and very quickly also taught Mi-pam-gya-tso his style of intonation and cadence, and so forth, of various rites.

At various times Mi-pam received from Jam-gön-gong-drül Lo-drö-ta-ye[46] instructions on the common topics of knowledge such as Chandragomin's Sanskrit grammar[37] and the five euphonic combinations,[38] through the study of which he was able to understand, without being taught, other texts of Sanskrit grammar, such as Anubhū-tisvarūpāchārya's *Sarasvatī's Grammar Sūtra*,[49] Sarvarvarman's *Kalāpasūtra*,[40] and so forth. His teacher told him that he must have been an Indian paṇḍita over many

lifetimes in order to be able to understand Sanskrit grammar so well—likely being the only person in Tibet at that
time who could understand it so fully—and that in order
to help sentient beings he should study medicine. So, he
studied the four medical tantras, including how to use purified mercury in medicine.

From the same master he received the collections of
exalted activities of pacification, increase, subjugation, and
control of Black Mañjushrī Lord of Life,[41] a Ñying-ma
Highest Yoga Tantra deity, and so forth together with all
of the quintessential instructions for maturation and release involved in those practices. Once this transmission
was complete, Jam-gön-gong-drül Lo-drö-ta-ye announced
that, like a father to his child, he would bestow on Mi-
pam-gya-tso the full scope of Ñying-ma doctrines, including ritual activities and quintessential instructions that he
had acquired in direct transmission including those never
written down.

From many spiritual guides such as Padmavajra,[42] pre-
ceptor of Dzok-chen Monastery, Mi-pam-gya-tso heard
endless cycles on Sūtra, Mantra, and the topics of knowledge. He did not just leave them as something heard but
put them into practice effectively. The causes—these being
the potentialities of auspicious lineage from having trained
well and having familiarized with these practices over
countless lives—were thoroughly activated by the condition of the power of lamas' transference of magnificent
blessings of compassion and thought. Through this he
comprehended all modes of profound and vast essentials of
Buddha's scriptures without contradicting the four reliances[43] in the manner of the four correct reasonings.[44] By
attaining dominion with regard to the appearance of self-
arisen qualities equal to space, he attained the eight great
treasures of confident exposition.

When the spiritual guide Ju-wön Jik-may-dor-je[45]

bestowed on him the oral reading-transmission of the root text of the *Condensed Perfection of Wisdom Sūtra,* he immediately was able to generate understanding regarding the features of the view of the Perfection of Wisdom, such that from merely reading texts in that field there was nothing he could not understand. Ju-wön Jik-may-dor-je conversed with Mi-pam-gya-tso about the text, and seeing that Mi-pam was more skilled than he was in the difficult and profound points, he asked Mi-pam-gya-tso to teach him those profound points, which he did. Ju-wön Jik-may-dor-je said, "Though I have studied until old age, I have not heard anything better than what I have heard from him. His teaching is the best." Even nowadays, among Ñying-mas Mi-pam's commentary on the perfection of wisdom is considered to be the best and the clearest.

Bum-šar Ge-šhay Nga-wang-jung-ñe[46] bestowed on Mi-pam-gya-tso an oral reading-transmission of Chandra-kīrti's *Supplement to (Nāgārjuna's) "Treatise on the Middle."* Mi-pam told the Ge-šhay that except for a reading-transmission he need not trouble himself; and so as soon as the Ge-šhay finished, he quizzed Mi-pam on the difficult terms and meanings of the text, the relevant commentaries on particular topics, and their explanations. The Ge-šhay was amazed, praising him in the presence of his retinue, declaring that even though he had gained the name "Ge-šhay (doctor professor)," he did not have even a mere portion of the understanding that Mi-pam-gya-tso had.

From the great professor of Ngor, Lo-de-wang-bo,[47] who was also a student of Jam-yang-kyen-dzay-wang-bo and famous among the Ša-gya School, Mi-pam received a reading-transmission on the *Treasury of Reasoning on Valid Cognition*[48] by Ša-gya Paṇḍita.[49] From Lo-de-wang-bo's manager, Padma,[50] he received the Five Doctrines of Mai-treya and Asaṅga's *Grounds of Bodhisattvas* and so forth. After these, Mi-pam-gya-tso taught at length to the great

Śa-ḡya scholars of this monastery the five great treatises of Maitreya, Chandrakīrti's *Supplement to (Nāgārjuna's) "Treatise on the Middle,"* and so forth. They considered him to be a very bright young scholar who had an extraordinary capacity to explain both words and meaning; at Śa-ḡya monasteries there was no one who could rise in debate against him. He was also invited to lecture at places of study of all of the orders of Tibetan Buddhism within Kam Province, whereby he became renowned as a highly developed scholar, at the peak of fame among all scholars in Kam.

When he was young, it was easy for him to study the texts of the New Translation Schools of Śa-ḡya, Ḡa-gyu,[51] and Ge-luk.[52] It seemed that there was nothing in their texts that he did not understand. He did have difficulties with certain Ñying-ma tantric texts, but still he determined that these were precious and valid pure transmissions and did not even for a moment generate any doubts or wrong ideas about Ñying-ma, figuring that the difficulties were due to his own lack of comprehension. Due to this, in time, when his meditation developed and his understanding and so forth advanced with age, he gained particularly strong ascertainment that these tantras and Padmasambhava's explanations contained supremely fantastic profound meaning.

At this stage of his full development he was called by his root lama Jam-ȳang-kyen-dzay-wang-bo to his monastery, where he advised Mi-pam-gya-tso to write many commentarial explanations that would set forth the Ñying-mas' own views with respect to these many topics. Thus, he wrote many commentaries setting forth Ñying-ma presentations of the view, meditation, and behavior. Because he composed these texts within putting great emphasis on Ñying-mas' own perspective, many scholars wrote texts attempting to counter what he had said. A great deal of controversy developed.

However, his intention was to further the Ñying-ma teaching at a time when it was quite weak; he did not intend to criticize other teachings. His hope and intention was, within Ñying-ma, to develop more persons who were interested in study, it being the case that within Ñying-ma most people, out of realization that life is impermanent and so forth, withdraw from the world and do not engage in an active way in such activities. Nevertheless, since he was emphasizing the Ñying-ma presentation on these topics, certain scholars from other orders, such as Ge-luk, got worked up about it.

Thus, he was carrying out the word of his lama, Jam-ȳang-kyen-dzay-wang-bo, who had advised him to write many commentaries, and he was seeking to encourage more Ñying-mas to develop in a scholarly way at a time when, as he said, the teachings of the Old Translation School were close to being a mere picture of a butter-lamp. He did not have any sense of showing absence of faith toward other schools. Mi-pam-gya-tso himself said, "You can look into my own compositions and see whether I have written them out of the pride of thinking that I was a very smart scholar, or whether they were written to help other beings."

Thinking that it might even be beneficial to those who were debating against what he had explained, he wrote careful and honest replies to their objections; he decided that he could from his own point of view perhaps discover points that he did not realize, or that he had understood improperly, and from others' points of view his responses might cause these scholars to realize points that they had not understood before, or had misunderstood. And he thought that if those scholars answered back, he might be able to use their answers like medicine. Therefore, he engaged in such written debates without an intention to be partisan in any sense, whether in terms of family line, area, or order of Tibetan Buddhism.

One of the greatest Ge-luk-ba scholars, Ba-ri Lo-sang-rap-šel,[53] wrote a two hundred page criticism of Mi-pam-gya-tso, called *Rap-sel's Response to Refutations*.[54] Many times they wrote criticisms back and forth, developing great respect for each other, because their compositions served to eliminate their qualms and so forth. This culminated in writing letters of praise of each other.

Also, in response to the Ge-luk master Drak-gar-drül-ğu Lo-sang-den-dzin-ñyen-drak[55] from Kam, Mi-pam-gya-tso wrote a shorter set of critical answers, called *Response to Objections Concerning the Chapter on Wisdom in (Shānti-deva's) "Engaging in the Bodhisattva Deeds": Sunshine Illumination*.[56]

While Mi-pam-gya-tso was writing a commentary on Dharmakīrti's *Commentary on (Dignāga's) "Compilation of Prime Cognition*,"[57] Ša-ğya Paṇḍita appeared to him in a dream in the guise of an Indian paṇḍita with a slightly hooked nose, asking him, "What could there be in the *Commentary on (Dignāga's) 'Compilation of Prime Cognition'* that you do not understand? It is just refutations and proofs." Ša-ğya Paṇḍita took Dharmakīrti's text and divided it into two parts, one half in one hand and one half in the other, saying, "If you put these two together, you will understand." In the dream Mi-pam-gya-tso put the two together, and immediately the book turned into a long sword, whereupon all knowables appeared in front of him. Ša-ğya Paṇḍita said, "If you wield this sword, it will penetrate all phenomena, all knowables, from forms to omniscient consciousnesses," and when Mi-pam wielded it, it cut through everything at once. From then, he was able to write commentary on Dharmakīrti's text just spontaneously.

When he looked into Guṇaprabha's *Aphorisms on Discipline,*[58] there were some points that he did not understand, but after reading once through the Translated Word of Buddha,[59] he reported that from his single reading of the thirteen volumes on discipline, he was able to understand everything in the *Aphorisms on Discipline* without impediment.

Concerning profound quintessential instructions and other matters such as the differences between earlier and later Tibetan schools, when he remained in solitary meditative retreat, performing the approximation of a deity by repeating mantra, understanding of these would spontaneously and vividly arise through the opening of channels of awareness and the blessings of his lamas and favored deities, without reading any texts or the like. He reported that due to this there was no way for him not to write these down.

On a particularly virtuous date, Jam-yang-kyen-dzay-wang-bo had volumes of Sūtra, Mantra, and topics of knowledge whose transmissions were rare and containing crucial points arranged on a large, high altar and made extensive offerings. He had Mi-pam-gya-tso sit on a platform-throne slightly lower than the altar. He announced, "I give you all of my authority with respect to holding, sustaining, and increasing the Buddha's teachings through explanation, debate, and composition. Make them shine in the world for a long time." Conducting a ritual called "Blazing Jewel of Lordship of Speech,"[60] he made him his regent, passing his transmission to him and bestowing a scroll-painting of white Tārā. He made a supplication for his long, steady life, which he himself composed in connection with Mi-pam-gya-tso's several names, and gave him many old representations of exalted body, speech, and mind. As a symbol of Mi-pam's power and stature, he took off his own long-eared hat and bestowed it on him, marking a marvelous event.

Later when speaking to others, Jam-ȳang-kyen-d̄zay-wang-b̄o announced that Mi-pam-gya-tso was the greatest of the scholars of that era on earth, since he knew all of the doctrines of the various orders of Tibetan Buddhism, and all of the topics of scholarship included in Sūtra and Mantra right through to the Great Completeness, as well as Sanskrit grammar, poetry, and so forth. Whereas some scholars might be better than him in a particular area, they did not have his depth and breadth of knowledge. Jam-gön-ḡong-d̄rül Lo-drö-ta-ye also praised him as a ma-hāpaṇḍita (a great scholar) and, though he was Mi-pam-gya-tso's lama, he requested from him instruction on his *Clear Exposition of the Text of (Dharmakīrti's) "Commentary on (Dignāga's) 'Compilation of Prime Cognition'"* and *Explanation of the Eight Pronouncements*[61] as well as others.

Ja-b̄a Do-n̄gak,[62] a [N̄ying-ma] scholar versed in the new traditions, criticized Mi-pam's commentary on the chapter on wisdom in Shāntideva's *Engaging in the Bodhisattva Deeds*, also known as the *Ketaka Jewel*. So, B̄a-d̄rül O-gyen-jik-me-chö-ḡyi-w̄ang-b̄o, supreme in scholarship, holiness, and adepthood, was made the judge, and those two debated in front of him. Though they contested all day and into the night, they were not able to come to any definite conclusion; they were over and over again debating about difficult points concerning Hearers' entry to the Great Vehicle path, a topic on which Indian paṇḍitas themselves could not come to any agreement, and other such difficult topics.

A lama in the audience named Rik-chok[63] asked B̄a-d̄rül O-gyen-jik-me-chö-ḡyi-w̄ang-b̄o to indicate who was the victor, since he and others considered both of them to be great scholars and thus found it difficult to determine who won. B̄a-d̄rül Rin-b̄o-chay responded, "I do not know how to determine the victor. It would not be proper if I indicated who is the better scholar. To cite a worldly proverb, 'A son is not praised by his father but by an enemy; a daughter is not praised by her mother but by the neighborhood.' If a lama praises his own student, it would be like a father who indeed would definitely praise his own son, or like a mother who, even if her daughter is not very pretty, will say, 'My daughter is very pretty and energetic.' In a similar way, if I indicated who was better, no one would believe me. However, Do-ngak's monks told me that during the early part of debate they clearly saw rays of light issue forth from the heart of Lama Mi-pam's image of Mañjushrī, his meditational deity, on the altar and enter into his heart and into mine. From that you can understand."

At one point Ba-drül Rin-bo-chay intervened saying, "Why don't you leave this topic, since even the Indian scholars could not settle it? This is to be settled by natural reasoning, and thus it will not help to debate about it." They were both probably very thirsty at that point, and tea was brought to them. Over tea, Ba-drül Jik-me-chö-gyi-wang-bo remarked, "Ja-ba Do-ngak has written a text on the basis, path, and fruit of the Nying-ma Great Completeness. Some people praise it, but others criticize it; it would be better for you two to talk about this while taking tea."

Mi-pam-gya-tso immediately rose up to debate, saying, "This text is not suitable at all, never mind the path and the fruit, he could not even get the basis right."[64] In just several minutes Mi-pam-gya-tso was able to defeat Ja-ba Do-ngak in debate, at which point Ba-drül Rin-bo-chay declared to Ja-ba Do-ngak, "You have been defeated. Such faulty reasoning would ruin the path; it would be best to burn the text."

Ba-drül Rin-bo-chay added, "That is enough debate. Bring them some food." And so, as Ja-ba Do-ngak was eating his food, he was thinking of the tough spot that he was in—that his root lama had his book burned and not Mi-pam-gya-tso's—and tears streamed down his cheeks. The many monastics and yogis who had gathered to listen to the debate noticed that he was crying, and he became famous throughout the two eastern provinces of Tibet, Kam and Am-do, as the person whom Mi-pam made cry.

Ja-ba Do-ngak was the only person who actually met in debate with Mi-pam-gya-tso. Ge-luk-ba scholars from great centers of learning sent essays of criticism against Mi-pam's positions, but did not actually come to debate. It is reported that, later on, a Ge-shay was sent from Lo-sel-ling College of Dre-bung Monastic University to find Mi-pam-gya-tso and debate against him, but when they met, the Ge-shay talked with him without actually debating, later reporting that he was a very amazing lama. Much later, Den-ma Rin-bo-chay (the predecessor of the present one) upon hearing this was provoked and decided that he would go and debate with Mi-pam-gya-tso. However, he arrived when Mi-pam-gya-tso was about to die, and so they never got a chance to debate.[65]

After the debate with Ja-ba Do-ngak, Mi-pam-gya-tso went into meditative retreat in the Tiger Den of Gar-mo in Kam Province for a period of thirteen years. He reported that during that period he was never distracted from the yogic approximation of Black Mañjushrī Lord of Life, due to which all signs of achievement described in the texts arose. At one point, he went to see his lama, Jam-yang-kyen-dzay-wang-bo, who asked him, "How is your practice going in retreat?" Mi-pam-gya-tso answered, "When I studied the great texts, I understood them thoroughly, but I am concerned that in meditative retreat on my favored deity I will not bring the stage of generation to fulfillment, so I am taking great care in practicing it with energy and earnestness."

Jam-ȳang-kyen-dzay-wang-bo remarked, "Doing it that way is very difficult. As the omniscient Long-chen-rap-jam[66] said, 'Without doing anything, remain in your natural face.' That is what I did, and though I did not see anything with white flesh and a ruddy complexion that could be called 'the face of the mind,' I do not have the slightest of worries about death," and he laughed. Mi-pam-gya-tso took this as advice that he should now just cultivate the view of the Great Completeness. Later, he reported that this was very helpful to him.

With respect to his meditative achievements, through putting penetrative focus on important points in the vajra body during the completion stage of Highest Yoga Tantra, he purified most of the movements of karmic winds in the central channel, and his mind experienced the metaphoric and actual clear lights—the great bliss of the fundamental innate pristine wisdom—induced by the four joys and four empties. In particular, in dependence upon the Great Completeness yoga of breakthrough-to-essential-purity and spontaneous leap-over,[67] he arrived at direct perception of the noumenon,[68] attaining mastery over appearance and behavior as the sport of exalted body and exalted wisdom.

Through the force of purifying his internal channels and essential constituents into a cloud-wheel of syllables, exalted knowledge arisen from meditation burst forth from the expanse. By cultivating the view of the Great Completeness, he received texts within the expanse of thought, and he wrote them down. He did not have to do research, comparing this and that; expositions just naturally emerged from the expanse of reality.

However, he did not announce that these were Thought-Treasures, texts received in thought-transmission from the great expanse, but just said that they were his compositions. Thirty-two such books—just as a Buddha has thirty-two marks—were published in Kam, but there

are also many notes as well as a number of texts about
black and white astrology, medicine, and Sanskrit that
were never published and have not arrived in India. He
expressed the hope that the collection of thirty-two texts
would serve as a way of reviving and furthering the Ñying-
ma teaching, which had come to a point of deterioration
like a person about to die.

In the Water Mouse Year (1912) on the thirteenth day
of the first month (Friday, March 1), he left meditative
retreat, and on the twenty-first, as a sign that he was about
to die, he called his manager and asked him to bring a
piece of paper. He wrote that after dying he would assume
the aspect of a youthful Bodhisattva in the pure land of
Manifest Joy in the east. "With an attitude of great compassion for all sentient beings throughout space I will remain helping sentient beings as long as there is space. This
is my promise."

It appears that Mi-pam-gya-tso was sick during a great
deal of his life, and so he wrote, "An exponent of the Buddhist doctrine at this time of the five ruinations was I, suffering continuously for seventeen years from a chronic disease of the channels. Even though I have suffered a great
deal from disease until now, I have stayed here in this land,
but I think that now it would be better to die, and thus I
will write my will." Thus he wrote his will and gave it to
his manager, Lama Ö-šel, who himself was a great scholar,
to hide.

Near the time of his death he said to his manager, "I
am not an ordinary being. I am a Bodhisattva who
through the power of wishes took rebirth in order to help
sentient beings. What I was seeking to do was to help the
Buddha's teaching, and especially to help the teaching of
the Great Completeness, but in general since the Ñying-
mas are of very little merit, they undergo a great deal of
harm from interrupting factors, and thus through the

dependent-arising of certain circumstances I have had to suffer a lot physically and have not been able to achieve the level of assistance that I was seeking to bring. However, I have mostly achieved what I wanted to do in terms of commentaries, even though I have not been able to write an extensive general-meaning commentary on Madhyamaka, as I had hoped, but that does not matter much. However, if I were able to finish writing on the fundamental mind in accordance with my wish to fully express my own thought about it, I think that it would be of immense benefit to all of the orders, Old and New, but I have not able to finish this." His point was that he had written a considerable amount on the topic of the fundamental mind, but had not completed it.

Then he announced, "I will not be taking actual rebirth in this world any more, because outlying barbarians will arrive and make a mess out of the teaching. Therefore, I will remain just in pure lands but will send emanations to impure lands. It is the responsibility and wish of Bodhisattvas in pure lands to send forth inconceivable emanations to impure lands to help sentient beings in whatever way would be suitable to tame them, and thus innumerable emanations will appear."

That evening he indicated that his long-term illness did not seem to be with him any more, that he had been cured of it, not feeling any pain, and most of the mistaken appearances of cyclic existence had disappeared, and he was perceiving pure appearances of rainbows, drops, exalted bodies, pure lands, and so forth associated with the meditative process of leap-over. He had instructed his manager not to let people into his room, but now he said, "Let them all in," and he gave to each of them instructions on how they should practice and made prayer-wishes for each of them. Those who had come for audience told him that he was not very old and should stay and help others.

He said, "No, it is definite that I am going to die. I am not going to take rebirth. One of my emanations will proceed to Shambhala in the north." In his sixty-seventh year, on the twenty-ninth day of the fourth month of the Water Mouse Year (June 14, 1912), he assumed meditative posture, his mind entering into equipoise in the primordial basal expanse.

Mi-pam-gya-tso had a great many famous students,[69] the most renowned being his manager, but during the course of his life he did not establish a big monastery or have many images constructed, and in the latter part of his life he stayed entirely in a hermitage in Kam, composing texts and so forth. As he said in his will, he considered the Three Cycles on Fundamental Mind to be very important, and although he was unable to complete them in the way he wanted, he had set them down in a rough way, which were then edited by Shay-chen Gye-dzal.[70]

Just as Mi-pam-gya-tso felt that his exposition on fundamental mind would be helpful to scholar-practitioners of all orders of Tibetan Buddhism, I also, hoping that it will be of use to those interested in the nature of reality, will comment in this book on the difficult points and so forth of the first of the Three Cycles on Fundamental Mind.

Khetsun Sangpo Rinbochay
Founder and Head, Nyingmapa Wishfulfilling Center
Bouda, Nepal

*The Meaning of Fundamental Mind,
Clear Light, Expressed in Accordance
with the Transmission
of Conqueror Knowledge-Bearers:
Vajra Matrix*

By Mi-pam-gya-tso

With Commentary
By Khetsun Sangpo Rinbochay

In the Introduction, Khetsun Sangpo Rinbochay's expansive oral commentary is at the margin, and Mi-pam-gya-tso's text is indented. After that, the four chapters that form the body of the text are at the margin, and oral comments on difficult points are in footnotes.

Introduction

Countering Unfavorable Forces

Because this is Secret Mantra, listeners should attain initiation beforehand. However, if the circumstances for this have not come together, it would be good, for the sake of avoiding interrupting factors, to recite the one-hundred-syllable mantra:

Om vajrasatva, samayam anupālaya, vajrasatva, tvenopatishtha, dṛdho me bhava, sutoshyo me bhava, suposhyo me bhava, anurakto me bhava, sarva-siddhiṃ me prayachchha, sarva-karmasu cha me chittam shrīyam kuru, hūm ha ha ha ha hoḥ, bhagavan-sarva-tathāgata-vajra, mā me muñcha, vajrī bhava, mahāsamaya-satva, āḥ hūm phaṭ. (Om Vajrasattva,[71] keep [your] pledge. Vajrasattva, reside [in me]. Make me firm. Make me satisfied. Fulfill me. Make me compassionate. Grant me all feats. Also, make my mind virtuous in all actions. Hūm ha ha ha ha hoḥ, all the supramundane victorious Ones-Gone-Thus, do not abandon me, make me indivisible. Great Pledge Being, āḥ hūm phaṭ.)

This should be done at least every day before going to sleep at night.

Or, you could recite the mantra *om vajrasatva hūm.* In each of the syllables, there is one of the five lineages of Vajrasattva:

om is the white Vajrasattva
vajra is the red Vajrasattva
sa is the yellow Vajrasattva
tva is the green Vajrasattva
hūm is the blue Vajrasattva.

Accumulating at least a hundred repetitions of this mantra every day helps in purifying karmic obstructions. Vajrasattva contains all of the hundred lineages. If you are able to recite this mantra for at least one rosary each day, whatever ill deeds you have accumulated will not increase in force. This is Secret Mantra and, unlike Sūtra, requires taking many pledges and so forth beforehand; I suggest the recitation of this mantra every day, especially if you have not received initiation.

Imagine a lotus on the top of your head, and upon it imagine Vajrasattva yab-yum;[72] both male and female are white. Then imagine that at the heart of the male is a small flat moon disc, the size of a mustard seed, that has the hundred-syllable mantra around its edge. The letters of the mantra are standing upright, facing inward, circling around the edge.

Take your recitation of *om vajrasatva hūm* as a prayer to it—to activate it. Just as when a child cries to its mother, the mother powerlessly gives what is required, so here through the repetition of the mantra the minds of Vajrasattva yab-yum are stirred. As you recite the mantra, this stirs them, and the letters set around the edge of the moon begin melting like butter put out in the sun, flowing from both male and female. The continuum of melted ambrosia comes down into the lotus on the top of your head, then into the stem of the lotus which is four finger widths inside your head. These drops gradually fill your entire body.

As this nectar comes into your body, imagine that all of your sicknesses, ill-deeds, obstructions, and so forth in the form of various types of black awful things go down to the bottom of your body and then out through the lower holes and hair pores. All of the evil spirits and so forth that are in you come out in the form of black scorpions, toads, and so on.

Then imagine that all of the factors that would cause interruption to you, bringing havoc to your life and so forth, manifest as a red bull, down nine stories below the earth, that has its mouth open upwards. Imagine that all beings to whom you owe a debt incurred over your beginningless lifetimes—beings whose flesh you have used, debts of money that you have not paid back, and so forth—all of these beings gather in a great assembly with their mouths gaping upwards. Imagine that all of these awful black substances that have come out of your body—scorpions, toads, and the like—transform into whatever any of these beings want, such that they get whatever they want.

Then imagine that every being has a Vajrasattva yab-yum on top of his or her head and is engaged in the same process of purifying ill-deeds and obstructions.

For the purification of ill-deeds you need to have four powers. The first power is that of the basis, which in this case is Vajrasattva yab-yum. The second power is contrition for ill-deeds you have done in the past: "I have done such and such terrible things; I will not do them anymore." This is the power of wiping out ill-deeds. The third power is that of restraint, feeling that in the future you will keep from any of these ill-deeds. The fourth, the power of an antidote, is the recitation—in the long form—of the hundred-syllable mantra or, in the briefer form, of *oṃ vajrasatva hūṃ*. Recite it one-pointedly within visualizing the purification of ill-deeds, sicknesses, and so forth in the complete form that I have just described.

Do the recitation-visualization for one rosary length, that is, a hundred times, and then change your visualization. Imagine that Vajrasattva has become extremely pleased, and is saying to you, "Child of good family, all of your ill-deeds and obstructions are purified." Then Vajrasattva and consort dissolve into light and melt into you, whereby you become Vajrasattva. Imagine that there is a blue *hūṃ* at the center of your heart—you do not need to visualize a moon disc as its base. There is a white *oṃ* in front, and on the right side is a red *vajra,* in the back a yellow *sa,* and on the left a green *tva.* Then imagine that all sentient beings have turned into Vajrasattvas and that the whole area surrounding you is not your usual local area but like the Eastern Pure Land of Vajrasattva. With a loud voice recite *oṃ vajrasatva hūṃ.*

Then the syllable *oṃ* turns into light and dissolves into *vajra; vajra* turns into light and dissolves into *sa; sa* turns into light and dissolves into *tva; tva* turns into light and dissolves into *hūṃ.* The syllable *hūṃ* dissolves into space like breath disappearing on a mirror; imagine that your mind is undifferentiable from this great emptiness. Stay in this state of immaculate vacuity as long as you can, and then when some conceptuality begins to stir in your mind, immediately recite, "Through the virtue of this may I turn into Vajrasattva and establish all sentient beings in the state of Vajrasattva."

Title of the Text

I will give an explanation of fundamental mind based on a text by Mi-pam-gya-tso.[73] Let us begin with his title, *The Meaning of Fundamental Mind, Clear Light, Expressed in Accordance with the Transmission of Conqueror Knowledge-Bearers: Vajra Matrix.* "Fundamental" means immutable, unchanging. Fundamental mind,[74] immutable mind,[75] clear light,[76] and noumenal mind[77] are synonymous. The topic of this book is the meaning of the ultimate clear light.

"Conqueror" refers to Buddhas, and "Knowledge-Bearers" means those holding the lineages. With respect to the word "transmission," this is a transmission of the Great Completeness,[78] which was passed from Ga-rap-dor-je,[79]

Jam-ɓel-šhay-ñyen,[80] and Shrī Sinha to Vairochana and Padmasambhava, and thereby to Tibet. Among Padmasambhava's greater students were King Tri-šong-day-d̄zen[81] and his twenty-five ministers, and it continues down to present lamas through to you today. There has been a transmission from lama to student, lama to student, without break. The main topic Mi-pam will discuss is the "vajra matrix," the essence of the vajra vehicles.

Homage

First Mi-pam pays homage to Mañjushrī in Sanskrit:

> *Namo gurumañjushrīye.*

There are three styles of preliminary homage: just in Sanskrit, in both Sanskrit and Tibetan, and just in Tibetan. This is an example of the first—an expression in Sanskrit. If we associate the two languages, *namo* is homage or bowing down (*phyag tshal*); *guru* is lama (*bla ma*); *mañjushrī* is Mañjushrī (*'jam dpal*); *ye* is to (*la*). Thus it means "Homage to the guru Mañjushrī."

You might wonder why a statement is made in an Indian language at the beginning of a Tibetan text. It is for the sake of gaining belief in the source of the teaching, that being in India. It is to indicate that texts composed in India and in Tibet do not differ in the quality of their topics expressed.

Next he makes an expression of worship:

> Obeisance with homage by way of knowledge
>   of one's own entity
> In which the supreme lama and special fa-
>   vored deity—
> Body of vajra essence that has come to be en-
>   dowed with the glory of smoothness—

> Are undifferentiable within the fundamental
> great bliss, mind-emptiness.

There are many ways of identifying a lama; here, because this is an occasion of Secret Mantra, it is the one who confers initiation. The word "lama," or "guru," is used only in Mantra, not in Sūtra. In the Sūtra system when vows are given, the reference is made to the abbot[82] or to the master[83] who confers the vows. Although you can find instances of the use of the word "lama" in the Sūtra system, these are cases of the Mantric term being brought over to Sūtra.

The syllable *la* (*bla*) in the term *lama* has the sense of that high place where all of the teaching of the Buddha abides; *ma* is to be understood as the mother of all these sentient beings who have been one's mother, the ultimate mother. The Sanskrit term *guru* (literally "heavy") means to have the weight of good qualities. How is it that a person comes to be weighty? This person has taken upon himself or herself the burden of freeing all sentient beings from suffering. The lama does that.

Among lamas there are the best, middling, and lower ones, and here the reference is to the best, or supreme, lama.

What is a *yidam*? A special favored deity. For those persons who cannot be tamed by a peaceful aspect, a lama appears in fierce aspect, this being a *yidam*. It is called a special deity because among the various *yidam* this is a deity that is particularly powerful with respect to taming trainees.

With regard to the phrase "glory of smoothness," in general "smooth" refers, for instance, to the smoothness of cloth, but here in this context it refers to the smoothness of not having any of the roughness of afflictive emotions. "Glory" refers to two factors: one is the realization that is one's own glory, because it is through realization that one becomes free from suffering, cyclic existence, and so forth; the other type of glory is that of compassion—it is a glory for others. "Has come to be endowed" is in the past tense, indicating that the one being talked about here has attained this.

In the phrase "body of vajra essence," "vajra" refers to immutability, the immutable noumenon, or final nature of phenomena. With respect to "mind-emptiness," it is by way of the artifice[84]—the activity—of knowledge on the one hand and ignorance on the other that one is either a Buddha or a sentient being. With knowledge, one is a Buddha; with ignorance, one is a sentient being wandering in cyclic existence.

"Fundamental" here refers to the immutable noumenon, the nature of phenomena. Ša-ġya Paṇḍita's[85] Tibetan spelling book says that emptiness is a *ga nyug,* that is, a *nyug* with a *ga* prefix—this is the word "fundamental" (*gnyug ma*)—and he says that bamboo (*snyug ma*) is *sa nyug*—it is spelled with a *sa* superscription. [The two words sound alike, but are spelled differently and have different meanings.]

"Within great bliss" means within great bliss that is immutable because, unlike ordinary happiness that is present one moment and gone in another moment, this is unchanging. "Within" means that one remains continuously within this like the current of a river. "Undifferentiable" means that one is realizing the nature of one's own mind as undifferentiable from the qualities enumerated above. From among types of homage, the best is with the view of reality, within knowledge.

What is the meaning of "homage"? It means that one is seeking the highest enlightenment of a Buddha through uprooting, or completely eradicating, the two obstructions—the afflictive obstructions and the obstructions to omniscience. That is a general meaning of "homage." Here, in particular, one should understand the nature of one's own mind, the reality of one's own mind; this is the highest form of homage. "Obeisance" indicates that one is bowing down to the feet—with homage to one's lama and the transmission of this view.

Aim of the Composition

Mi-pam continues:

> Concerning this, the essentials of all doors of doctrine of the Great and Small Vehicle—inconceivably set forth in accordance with the dispositions, faculties, and thoughts of trainees in the ten directions and three times through the inconceivable secrecy of speech of the One-Gone-Thus—are included in the two vehicles, cause and effect.

"Concerning this" means with respect to the contents of that expression of worship just explained. "One-Gone-Thus"[86] alternatively could be "One-Gone-to-Bliss."[87] "Secrecy of speech" refers only to Secret Mantra. One could include Mantra within the sets of manifest knowledge of the Sūtra system from among the three scriptural divisions—sets of discourses, sets of discipline, and sets of manifest knowledge, but here "secrecy of speech" refers to just Secret Mantra. "Inconceivable" here means that this secrecy of speech of the Ones-Gone-Thus is beyond the verbalization and realization of our mistaken minds.

"The ten directions" are north, east, south, west, northeast, southeast, northwest, southwest, zenith, and nadir. "The three times" are past, present, and future. "Trainees" are those who have the lot of being trained by the Buddha's teaching. The Buddha set forth teachings in accordance with the dispositions, faculties, and thoughts of trainees; to those of low interest he set forth the low vehicle; to those of middling interest he set forth the middling vehicle; and to those of great interest he set forth the Great Vehicle. "Doors of doctrine" refers to, for instance, the 84,000 bundles of doctrine that Buddha taught. The essentials of all these doors of doctrine are included in the two vehicles, cause and effect.

> Furthermore, the thought of the perfection of wisdom, which is the peak of all views of the causal path of the perfections, meets back to the sphere of reality[88] devoid of all extremes of proliferation,[89] emptiness endowed with all supreme aspects, known by oneself individually.

The causal vehicle is the vehicle of the path of the perfections—the six perfections of giving, ethics, patience, effort, concentration, and wisdom. The peak of all of the views of the path of the perfections, that is, of the causal vehicle, is the thought of the perfection of wisdom. Then Mi-pam speaks of that which is devoid of all of the extremes of proliferation. One way of taking proliferation is set forth at the beginning of Nāgārjuna's *Treatise on the Middle,* when he speaks of that which is free from the eight proliferations—production, cessation, annihilation, permanence, coming, going, sameness, and difference. Also Chandrakīrti's *Supplement to (Nāgārjuna's) "Treatise on the Middle"* speaks of a mode of subsistence free from the proliferations of the four extremes of production—production from self, production from other, production from both self and other, and causeless production. The Middle Way view is called a view having no assertions, devoid of all such extremes. As Nāgārjuna says in his *Refutation of Objections,*[90] "Because I have no assertions, I do not have any fault."

What is this view devoid of all assertions? It is the sphere of the nature of phenomena, the sphere of reality.

This sphere of reality is identified as emptiness endowed with all supreme aspects. Because it is free from all assertions—of all directions of north, south, east, west, and so forth—it is emptiness, but it is endowed with the supreme of all aspects. It is understood individually by oneself.

When Buddha's son, Rāhula, made a praise of the mother, the perfection of wisdom, he called it inconceivable, unfabricated, the perfection of wisdom, unproduced, unceasing, the entity of space itself, that which is realized individually by oneself, the perfection of pristine wisdom. And because all Buddhas of the three times—past, present, and future—are born from it, he paid obeisance to the mother of the Buddhas of the three times having all of these qualities. Maitreya's *Ornament for Clear Realization* describes emptiness as the mother of all Buddhas because if persons realize emptiness, they can become Buddhas, and if they do not realize emptiness, there is no way at all to become a Buddha. That is the reason why the perfection of wisdom is treated as the mother of all Buddhas. Just as a river meets back to, or derives from, a snow mountain, so the view derives from this which is realized individually.

> The finality of the thought of all profound, resultant mantric tantras meets back to this which is described in the *Compendium of the Thought of the Sūtras*[91] as "The sphere of the mind, the natural clear light, the suchness of Secret Mantra."

The Mantra system is profound in that it is deep and cannot to be understood immediately. The reason why Mantra is called resultant, the effect, is that whereas Sūtra paths work on the causes of enlightenment, Mantra paths are based on the effect. With respect to the tantras, there are many different ways of enumerating them—64,000 tantras and so forth—and Mi-pam is about to talk about the ultimate thought of all the tantras.

There are two *Compendium of the Thought of the Sūtras,* one related with the Mind-Only School and one related with the Great Completeness. This is the one from the Great Completeness.

As long as you cannot make a difference between mistaken mind and unmistaken mind, you cannot understand anything that is said here. What are we accustomed to? Night and day, during the six periods of an entire day, what we are accustomed to is mistaken mind. In all of our activities—the agents and objects with which we are involved every day—it is as if the mind of reality, the reality of the unmistaken mind, is dormant, and we are engaging in activities from within mistaken mind. Performing all of these actions, or works, are the six main consciousnesses and fifty-one mental factors. Who indicated that these are mistaken minds? Buddha said in the *Descent into Laṅkā Sūtra,*[92] "Minds and mental factors have the aspect of an exaggeration of the three realms," the desire realm, form realm, and formless realm.

Therefore, beginners initially learn about the conventionalities and then use those conventionalities as means for ascending to the higher level of the ultimate—like the steps of stairs. If you do not train originally very finely in the presentations of conventional phenomena, then when you come to the difficult level of the ultimate, you cannot understand anything. When you become very skilled in conventional phenomena, then you can, through gradual changes in perspective, quickly understand the ultimate.

This is why Buddha, upon becoming enlightened, first taught the four noble truths and then taught the Great Vehicle. If he had taught the doctrines of the Great Vehicle in the beginning, no one would have understood. Since almost all of the things we are doing and all of what we are thinking are bogged down in mistaken mind, we have to study conventional mistaken mind, and then, when we turn to the ultimate, we can give up entirely all of these activities lodged in the mistaken mind. The situation of our mind now is that we are so used to mistaken mind that we cannot understand what ultimate mind is.

You might think that if you gave up all of these activities of mistaken mind, you would become like a dead body. Hence, we instruct a person—who retreats to a solitary place on a mountain to cultivate this view of the Great Completeness—to think in the beginning that it probably would be that if you cut off all of the activities of the mistaken mind you would end up being just like a dead body. After considering this for a while, the person comes to think that it could not be that the Supramundane Victor Buddha set forth something that was just like a dead body; there must be something beyond that, there must be an unmistaken reality. At that point the person begins seeking unmistaken reality.

How is it that mistaken mind overwhelms the unmistaken mind, unmistaken reality? To give an example, during the day when the sun is shining one does not see any stars and thus one would think that there are no stars at all, that they just plain do not exist. Just so, afflictive emotions shine so brightly and are so powerful that it is as if unmistaken reality, unmistaken mind, does not exist at all. When you seek out this unmistaken mind from within, you come to understand that there is an unmistaken mind—a reality of the mind—that does not die, that does not scurry after pleasure and pain. This mind that does not follow after pleasure and pain has a mode of being that is emptiness—but not an emptiness in the sense of an empty house or an empty vessel; rather, it is endowed with the inconceivable self-effulgence[94] of unmistaken reality, of pristine wisdom.

When you search for this that is beyond mistaken mind, mistaken mind just stops; gradually like dawn there comes to be a time when pristine wisdom manifests a little. With the beginning of dawn there is not just darkness but some light, and so it is when the self-effulgence, the self-color, the self-nature of the pristine wisdom shows itself a little; one generates a suspicion that there is wisdom beyond mistaken mind. As Āryadeva says, "When you generate doubt thinking that there might be such a reality, cyclic existence is torn to tatters."[94] How does cyclic existence come to be torn to tatters, or wrecked, made into a mess by doubt? For instance, if a table is wrecked, broken up, it cannot perform the function of a table; just so, when the self-effulgence of unmistaken pristine wisdom begins to dawn with this state of doubt, cyclic existence is wrecked and torn to tatters.

This mandala, this sphere, of the mind that is naturally clear light is suchness, only set forth in Secret Mantra and thus a distinguishing feature of Secret Mantra. Because whether one is caught in cyclic existence or not depends upon being able to differentiate between mistaken mind and unmistaken mind, great emphasis is put on this point, and that is why I have explained it in some detail.

> Therefore wise scholars (who, having completed vast hearing, thinking, and meditating, generated ascertaining knowledge from proper explanation through scriptures and reasonings by those perceiving the definitive meaning) or yogis (who, though they are not endowed with the great wisdom of having trained in hearing and thinking, generated conviction in accordance with having been introduced well to basic mind by a lama who, endowed with experience of the quintessential instructions, has totally mastered the essentials of basic mind, pristine wisdom) will not fall from

the essentials of the teaching with respect to the meaning of those two.

In the final phrase, "the meaning of those two," "those two" are the reality of the mind, which is unmistaken mind itself, and the clear light of Secret Mantra. In order to realize those two, it is necessary to engage in the beginning in vast hearing, then in the middle in vast thinking, and in the end in vast meditation. When you have brought vast hearing, thinking, and meditation to completion, you become a wise person. When Buddha taught, he set forth sūtras requiring interpretation for those persons who were not capable at that time of understanding the definitive Great Vehicle teachings, gradually leading them that way, eventually teaching them the definitive doctrines. "Scriptures" here refer to statements endowed with the blessings of the transmission. "Reasonings" (spelled *rigs* with the second suffix *sa*) is to be understood as rational reasoning. Although scribes have used different spellings and thus created some confusion, the word that means reasoning must have the secondary suffix (*rigs pa*), whereas when we speak about knowledge, basic mind, or basic knowledge (*rig pa*) of the unmistaken mind, it has no second suffix *sa*. One generates ascertaining knowledge from proper explanations, these explanations being by way of blessed statements and reasoning.

"Or" indicates a choice—you choose either the first way or the second way. Either in the mode of a great scholar you bring to full development hearing, thinking, and meditating, or even if you do not possess the great wisdom of having trained fully in hearing and thinking, you manifest from within—in the manner of a great meditator—the meaning of the reality of unmistaken mind. "Mastered" means that through gradually becoming accustomed to the reality of unmistaken mind, to emptiness, the person becomes fully enlightened such that realization is there from within. If you do not have a lama with experience such that he or she has mastery penetrating enlightenment, it is very difficult. The lama should be someone who through becoming accustomed to the reality of unmistaken mind has become enlightened.

Because the lama has experience, the lama can introduce and identify for the student how to meditate so that basic mind will become manifest. How does the lama introduce the student to reality? There are three phases— basis, path, and fruit. First, the lama introduces the student to the basis, the mind of clear light, the reality of unmistaken mind. At this time you must generate valid belief in the clear light; this depends upon the student's karmic obstructions, the karmic background, due to which there are varieties among students—some able to generate conviction, some not, as well as varieties in the strength of belief and so forth.

In any case, you must develop conviction to the level of valid cognition, realizing that since beginningless time all of your activities have been bogged down in mistakenness. When you generate conviction in the reality of unmistaken mind to the level of valid cognition, you become a yogi, one who has arrived at the natural state of reality. Yogis who have identified their own face, their own basic entity, will not stray from the essentials of the teaching.

> Otherwise, as sūtras and tantras prophesy, there are many who, having abandoned the profound meaning through dry analysis that seems so plentiful and so good, distribute quasi-doctrine for material gain, leading those of low merit and small intelligence on a perverse path at this time of the end of the era.

If you abandon the reality of unmistaken mind and engage

in many dry analyses that seem to you to be so good, so good, and are so multitudinous, so multitudinous, having no end, nothing will come of it. Once you become totally absorbed just in conventional verbiage, it is as if the profound ultimate reality has dried up. Then you use this quasi-religious doctrine as a means of gathering money, of getting things.

Such people of small mind and low merit at this degenerate time when the five degeneracies have set in, lead other people on a mistaken path, not directing them in the least to ultimate reality. This happens frequently; many people have ended up this way. Buddha prophesied in sūtras and in tantras that such would happen in the future—that there would be a time when people of low mind would sell religious doctrines in order to gain money.

> [Hence] those of good lot should seek the profound thought of the transmission of Conqueror Knowledge-Bearers with profound intelligence endowed with the four reliances.

Buddha spoke of four reliances:

1. Rely not on the person, but on the doctrine.
2. Within the doctrine, rely not on the words, but on the meaning.
3. Within the meaning, rely not on interpretable meanings, but on the definitive meaning.
4. Within the definitive meaning, rely not on mere consciousness, but on pristine wisdom.

People of good fortune should seek out the profound thought of the transmission of the Conqueror Knowledge-Bearers with profound intelligence endowed with these four reliances. If you do not understand it right away, you should keep working and working at it with such profound intelligence.

> It is not suitable to get involved with what is propounded with superficial logic, but due to the era, humans are weak in wisdom and effort; their merit and lot are small; virtuous spiritual guides who have perceived the ultimate are few; those who propound all sorts of conceptual fabrications are many; also the doctrine, having been polluted with their own mind, has become weaker and weaker like milk watered down to market, such that quasi-doctrines are very plentiful at this time of the degeneration of the teaching. Still, it is rare for anyone to know this.

The word "logic" (*rtog ge*) has two basic meanings, one is correct logic, and the other is wrong logic, but here the reference is to those who pay attention just to logic, without getting at the meaning. The term for "fabrications" (*zol ma*) also means deceit; it refers to just making up seemingly logical vocabulary and arguments that are not in the great treatises. Though it is not suitable to get involved with what is propounded with deceitful logic, due to the time, that is, due to the fact that we are in the era of the five degenerations, humans have little wisdom and little effort, and therefore are drawn into deceitful logic.

If you have great merit, you have the lot of being able to absorb much doctrine, but if you have little merit, you have the lot of being able to absorb only a little doctrine. Also, nowadays there are few virtuous spiritual guides who perceive the ultimate, the mode of subsistence of phenomena. And many people just make up things to say from their imagination, and end up just blabbing, fabricating their own vocabulary and polluting the doctrine with their own perspective, unable to leave the doctrines just as they are. For instance, when milk is sold, sellers often mix in water, making it very weak, and in the same way the doctrines have become weak with admixtures. This is a time when the doctrine has degenerated, like milk mixed with water, and thus there are many propounding quasi-doctrines, but there are very few who practice the real thing. At such a time it is rare to find anyone who knows the situation.

> Aside from those endowed with the best of accumulations of the collections [of merit and wisdom], ordinary beings cannot even understand the profound meanings. Even those who gain understanding from deliberate earnest analysis and investigation are few.

The profound meanings of Mantra are to be realized by those who have great accumulations of the collections of merit and wisdom. Aside from people who have the highest level of the accumulations of merit and wisdom, ordinary people cannot even understand these doctrines. And there are only a few who are able to gain understanding from analyzing and investigating intensely and earnestly.

> At such a time when, despite the fact that the modes of appearance to the ordinary conceptual awarenesses of the short-sighted are contradictory with the innermost profound meaning, [people] voluntarily take up [these superficial, false modes of appearance] with enthusiasm—like a dog coming upon lungs—thinking, "These immediate things are it!" and discard the profound, saying, "The profound meaning cannot be known." At such a time the very profound is difficult to fathom. Also, engagement of the mind in the essentials of the path—so meaningful when understood—is very rare.

People like us, who only know what is nearby them and do not know the more profound meanings, are called "short-sighted" (*tshur mthong*), those with limited sight. The mode of appearance to our ordinary conceptual aware-nesses is contradictory with the innermost profound meaning; and since we are limited to this superficial level, we are in a state of contradiction with the more profound. We immediately feel that this is all there is—that the su-perficial is all that exists.

When a dog comes upon lungs, it considers them to be so delicious it wants immediately to gobble them up; just the same, when we meet with any superficial teaching, whatever it is, we voluntarily sink ourselves into it or grab on to it. We discard the more profound, thinking that it is something unknowable. During such a era when we have discarded the more profound in favor of the more superfi-cial, indeed the profound is extremely difficult to plumb. When the profound is understood, it is very meaningful, but we live at a time when those who engage their minds in the essentials of the path, which when realized are very meaningful, are very rare.

> Therefore, I do not see much purpose in writing about this, but with the good intention that even at the end of an era it might help a few persons a bit, I will speak a little about central points con-cerning profound meanings very difficult to un-derstand that are a little clear to my mind due to the kindness of excellent lamas and profound scriptures.

Mi-pam-gya-tso is saying: I do not see much purpose in writing about such profundity; however, I think that at this time at the end of an era there definitely will be a few who will want to hear about such topics, and thus I think it might help. With this beneficial attitude, I will write about these profound meanings extremely difficult to understand. Through the kindness and force of the excellent lamas and the profound scriptures by the former great Conquerors, I will talk briefly about central meanings that appear somewhat clearly to my mind. The central meanings are the basis, path, and fruit, and here I will talk about the basis.

The Basal Clear Light

> About this, just this original (*ye thog*) basal clear light, the primordial (*gdod ma*) mode of subsistence, is the final reality of all phenomena. All appearances of cyclic existence and nirvāṇa shine forth from within it, and when they shine forth, there is not a single phenomenon that is other than continuously abiding in it.

Ye has the sense of "original," and *thog ma* means "first," so the reference here is to the original basal clear light. The basis, here in the system of the Great Completeness, is not just a non-existence, or a mere negative, but is the clear light that is the primordial subsistence of things. It is the final reality of all phenomena.

From within the basal clear light, all appearances of cyclic existence and nirvāṇa shine forth. And when they shine forth from within the mind of clear light, they do not become separate from it but are like the effulgence of that mind of clear light. Thus there is no phenomenon other than ones that remain abiding within that mind of clear light when it shines forth.

> Since this is the final place of release, it is called "the body of attributes that is the ultimate mode of subsistence." When finally the adventitious obstructions as well as their predispositions are

purified, it is called "the nature body endowed with the two purities," the final true cessation in the supreme vehicle.

Because this basal mind of clear light is the final place of release, it is what is called "the body of attributes that is the ultimate mode of subsistence." The body of attributes is complete within this basal mind of clear light. Thus, what defiles it and prevents its manifestation? An example of this situation is the sun and the clouds: the sun is the basal mind of clear light, and the clouds are our own adventitious and temporary predispositions blocking realization, or manifestation, of the sun. When we are unable to see the sun, we think that only clouds exist; just so, due to our predispositions we think that those things that come forth from these predispositions are all that there is.

When these adventitious predispositions and obstructions finally become purified, this basal mind of clear light itself is called "the nature body endowed with the two purities." This is not just the natural purity of being intrinsically free from defilements but also is the purity of being free from adventitious defilements. It is the final true cessation taught in the supreme vehicle. The supreme vehicle is the Vajra Vehicle and, within that, the Great Completeness.

> In that foundation, mistake and release are nondual. Just that foundation is the essential purity[95] from the viewpoint of being without any [conceptual and dualistic] proliferations and is spontaneity[96] in that it is not a mere emptiness like space but is self-luminous without partiality, not limited in its vastness, and not fallen into limitation. Since it is the source of all appearances of cyclic existence and nirvāṇa, it is called all-pervasive compassion.

Within that basis, that is to say, within that basal body of attributes, since it is primordially buddhafied, there is no such thing as error, and there is no such thing as release. Within that basis, error and release are non-dual, and thus it is the great natural equality.

Just that basis—the basal body of attributes of the mind of clear light—is the essential purity from the viewpoint of its being totally without any dualistic and conceptual proliferation. It is not just a mere emptiness like space or like an empty house, but has a self-arisen spontaneous nature of self-illumination. It is not partial, not limited anywhere in its extent—not ruptured due to being too vast—not fallen to any extreme.

Being the source of all appearances of cyclic existence and nirvāna, it is the place from which they arise. Because it pervades everything right through Buddhahood, it is called all-pervasive compassion.

> In the doctrinal vocabulary of the tantras of the Great Completeness, it is the triply endowed pristine wisdom residing as the basis. Similarly, in the sūtras and tantras, it is called the "sphere"[97] and "emptiness"[98] from the viewpoint of being without observation of marks and being devoid of all aspects of proliferation; "self-arisen pristine wisdom" from the viewpoint of luminous self-effulgence,[99] and "fundamental mind,"[100] "fundamental cognition,"[101] "natural mind of clear light,"[102] "mind-vajra,"[103] "that endowed with the space-vajra pervading space,"[104] and so forth due to not changing in any aspect.

In the tantras of the Great Completeness, it is said to be endowed with the three pristine wisdoms residing as the basis. The three are the mirror-like wisdom, the wisdom of the sphere of reality, and the wisdom of individual realization. From among the Buddha's five wisdoms, here Mi-pam-gya-tso mentions only three because he is speaking about the clear light that is the basis, rather than when manifested at Buddhahood as the five wisdoms. The remaining two, the wisdom of equality and the wisdom of the accomplishment of activities, are attained with Buddhahood and are endowed with the two purities— natural purity and purity of adventitious defilements.

In the sūtras and the tantras it is called "sphere and emptiness." It is called "sphere" from the viewpoint of being without observation of any marks, being devoid of all aspects of proliferation, such as production, cessation, coming, going, and so forth, as mentioned at the beginning of Nāgārjuna's *Treatise on the Middle,* and for the same reason it is called "emptiness." It is devoid of all marks and signs, which are like smoke being the sign indicating the presence of fire.

From its factor of luminous self-effulgence, it is called "self-arisen pristine wisdom." And due to its not changing in any aspect, it is called "fundamental mind." In other texts it is called "fundamental cognition" and "natural mind of clear light." From the viewpoint of its immutability, it is called "mind-vajra" since it does not undergo any change. The mind-vajra pervades wherever space is present, and thus this basal mind of clear light is called "that endowed with the space-vajra pervading space."

> Though it is taught with such synonyms, all of them are not different in fact from only the nondual sphere of reality and pristine wisdom, the noumenon of the mind, the ultimate mode of subsistence, the vajra-like mind of enlightenment itself. Therefore, although it is called the "sphere of reality," it is not to be understood as a mere empty sphere but as emptiness endowed with all supreme

aspects, without any conjunction with or disjunction from luminosity. Though it is called "self-arisen," it is to be understood not as a compounded awareness—endowed with marks, a subject realizing emptiness within a division of object and subject—but as having a luminous nature without even a particle of any mark to be designated as compounded.

The different names come by way of emphasizing different qualities. Though it is taught with various terms, all of them are not different in fact from only the vajra-like mind of enlightenment, the noumenon of the mind, or ultimate mode of subsistence, the non-duality of the sphere of reality and pristine wisdom. Although there are these many different names, their meanings do not exist as separate factualities; it is just this vajra-like ultimate mind of enlightenment, the mode of subsistence of things.

It is called "the sphere of reality," but it is not be understood as just a mere empty sphere. Rather, it is luminous. The sphere does not come together with luminosity or separate from luminosity, but is beyond coming together with anything and separating from anything. It is emptiness endowed with all supreme aspects.

It is called "self-arisen pristine wisdom," but it is not some kind of subject that is the counterpart of an object—not a mere awareness that is a subject realizing emptiness from within a division into subject and object. It is immutable mind, not to be confused with compounded mind having marks. Although it has a luminous nature, it does not have even a particle of a mark that is to be designated as compounded; it is uncompounded.

> Within the Great Completeness, in the mind-class and so forth it is called "the mind of enlightenment"; in the expanse-class and so forth it is called

"sphere of reality"; in the quintessential-instruction-class it is called "pristine wisdom"; in the Perfection of Wisdom Sūtras it is called "sphere of reality"; and in most mantric tantras it is called "fundamental mind." In such statements there are different names due to the force of certain needs, but the meaning to be understood is the union of basic knowledge and emptiness, the actual pristine wisdom that is what is being characterized, the mode of subsistence of all phenomena. Hence, it is the primordial innate pristine wisdom.

In the Great Completeness there are three classes of teachings—mind-class, expanse-class, and quintessential-instruction-class. In the mind-class, it is called "mind of enlightenment." In the expanse-class, it is called "sphere of reality." In the class of the teaching known as quintessential instruction, it is called "self-arisen pristine wisdom." In the Perfection of Wisdom texts—the perfection of wisdom being the mother that gives rise to all Buddhas—it is called "sphere of reality." And in most mantric tantras, it is called "fundamental mind." Due to the force of certain circumstances, needs, purposes, and intentions there are different names, but when you come down to it, what is to be understood is a union of basic knowledge and emptiness, the actual pristine wisdom; this is what is being characterized. Since it is the final mode of subsistence of all phenomena, it is the primordial innate pristine wisdom.

Not being produced through the fluctuations of the predispositions of the three appearances, it is naturally flowing noumenon.[105] Because of being devoid in all ways from the pangs of suffering of these mutations, it is designated "great bliss."

There are many different identifications of the three

appearances. In texts on death, intermediate state, and rebirth, the three appearances are identified as appearance, increase, and near-attainment—the minds of vivid white appearance, vivid red or orange increase of appearance, and vivid black near-attainment, called the minds of white, red, and black appearance.

In the vocabulary of the Ša-gya system, the three appearances are identified as 1) impure appearance, 2) visionary appearance, and 3) pure appearance. Applying this division of three appearances to the basis, path, and fruit, the basis is the impure appearances that you are currently perceiving. Then, when you endeavor at the spiritual path and so forth, there are visionary appearances. When you advance and have purified the visionary appearances, there is pure appearance of the state of the effect in which everything is limitless purity—these being natural appearances that come from meditating on emptiness.

> As long as you have not identified actual pristine wisdom, all cases of mental imputations and apprehensions in which you have a sense of:
>
> - a subject that is a compounded awareness and an object that is uncompounded mere emptiness
> - a changeable compounded bliss
> - a similar [that is to say, changeable and compounded] sense of clarity and so forth
> - and a sense of not conceptualizing anything,
>
> you have not gone even in the direction of the definitive meaning, and consequently need to rely on the quintessential instructions of an excellent lama. Dry analysis without the orally transmitted quintessential instructions is, with respect to this topic [of the fundamental reality], like the blind looking at the sun.

If you remain with stale analysis, you are like a blind person trying to look at the sun.

(That concludes Khetsun Sangpo Rinbochay's expansive commentary on the Introduction. Hereafter, Mi-pam-gya-tso's text is at the margin, with comments by Khetsun Sangpo Rinbochay in footnotes.)

1. Vajra Matrix

While not fluctuating in any of the three times from this great clear light basal sphere, appearances of the two—cyclic existence and nirvāṇa—are ready to shine forth as appearances of the artifice [of basic mind] from within that mode of subsistence. However, at a time of non-realization and cyclic existence there are the various dual appearances of substrata as apprehended-objects and apprehending-subjects[106] due to not realizing the equality of the noumenon, and there are unequal appearances of self and other, good and bad, pleasure and pain, cyclic existence and nirvāṇa without any limit.

At the time of realized nirvāṇa, or purification, the noumenon that is the naturally flowing mode of subsistence is realized, whereby it is realized that all appearances whatsoever of substrata do not pass beyond that [basal mind of clear light]. Having realized [the great equality], it is realized that even though various aspects appear, all these have one taste in thusness, in the clear light sphere of reality without the marks of dualistic phenomena.[a] At that time, all phenomena of cyclic existence and nirvāṇa from forms on up shine forth as not having passed beyond the nature of buddhafication, primordially released.

Therefore, in terms of realizing the naturally pure noumenal mode of subsistence, all that appears is settled through the view as pure from the beginning, as naturally

---

a   Just as when rivers flow into the ocean they blend into one taste, so all of our conceptuality blends into one taste in realizing the noumenon. Oneself and others, as well as the different types of conceptuality, come all to have the one taste of reality. Even though all these things appear, they are one taste in suchness and are without the marks of duality.

pure primordially, as just buddhafied. Because this is established through reasoning concerning the noumenon,[107]
it is non-mistaken and non-delusive and hence is called the
correct view.

In the perspective of those having dualistic appearance, the two, impure sentient beings and pure Buddhas,
do not appear to be one, but appear to be different. No
one asserts that—in the perspective of those who perceive
in this way—all sentient beings are Buddhas, but what is
comprehended by mistaken awarenesses having dualistic
appearance does not damage non-dualistic pure awareness.
When yogis realize the noumenon of the mind, there is
not even a speck of the actual[108] eight collections of consciousness in the face of that realization; consciousness
itself dawns as pristine wisdom, and even all phenomena
similarly dawn as just naturally pure. When the noumenon
of the mind is taken to mind during the path without having realized the Great Completeness, the eight collections
of consciousness are apprehended in an ordinary aspect,
and the noumenon does not appear. Hence, such a person
does not have any way of knowing even preliminarily a
trace of where the uncompounded mind of clear light is.

Therefore, in terms of the exalted perception of one
who has thoroughly purified the defilements of obstructions as well as their predispositions in the mode of subsistence, all phenomena are just manifestly buddhafied in
that mode of subsistence. The *Monarch of Tantras: The
Vajrasattva Magical Net* says:[109]

> A Buddha does not find a phenomenon
> Other than Buddhahood.

Thus, the meaning indicated by the phrase "basic mind,
the clear light, the Great Completeness" is the noumenon
of the mind, self-arisen pristine wisdom, this which does
not become other than the sphere of reality, primordial

basal mode of subsistence, union, the great equality, the great uncompounded due to being immutable and not changing in the three times. However, there is no way that this could be understood as an impermanent momentary mind, which is a compounded subject, or as a non-thing, an uncompounded mere emptiness that is just an elimination of an object of negation by reasoning.

Therefore, this basal Great Completeness, or primordial basal clear light, great uncompounded union, is the final mode of subsistence of all phenomena, and it also is what is to be realized by the view. The *Tantra of Great Luminous Meaning Devoid of Proliferation* says:[110]

> From this uncompounded knowledge, primordially pure, this great unhindered vividness, all of cyclic existence and nirvāṇa appears; therefore, it is the pristine wisdom abiding as the basis.

and:

> In entity it is unmade, unfabricated, unpolluted, immutable, pure in nature, uncompounded, great luminous pristine wisdom, noumenon like space, emptiness renowned with the quality of a vajra, basic mind that is a non-thing, pure from the beginning, great unhindered vividness.

and:

> Basic mind that is luminous, empty, non-dual, and unhinderedly vivid.

and:

> When in all the scriptures of the tantras that I
>   have taught,
> I have expressed the vajra-like words
> Of "immutability" and "uncompoundedness,"

I have been explaining the great self-arisen wisdom.

and:

The immutable basis is primordially buddhafied;
it is the Supramundane Victor, the great Vajrad-
hara; hence, in the past it never experienced any
mistake, and also now is not mistaken, and fur-
thermore in the future will not be mistaken.

and:

The basis that is the meaning of reality is released
from the eight collections of consciousness, which
are concordant with it merely in that they are cognitive. Since it is without increase or decrease, it is
released from the mind-basis-of-all.[111] Since it is
without apprehended-object and apprehending-
subject, it is released from the mental consciousness, the sixth consciousness. Since it is without
production and cessation, it is released and re-
verted from the consciousnesses of the five doors.[a]

And on the occasion of setting forth examples to character-
ize this basis, [the *Tantra of Great Luminous Meaning Devoid of Proliferation*] speaks of being empty and pervasive
like space; undefiled like a crystal; immutable like a dia-
mond; giving rise to all blessings into magnificence, and
hence like a jewel; clear and unimpeded, like the essence of
the sun. And:

Opposite from ignorance and from matter, and
abiding as an entity of knowledge of reality, it is
knowledge. Due to being beyond causes and

---

[a]   The five sense consciousnesses—eye consciousness and so
forth.

conditions, it is self-arisen. Not having adventitiously arisen, it is pristine wisdom endowed with a nature of primordially abiding basic knowledge. It is the basis from which all of cyclic existence and nirvāṇa appear.

And it speaks at length about how that basis is called natural, spontaneously established Buddha; youthful encased body;[a] body of attributes; nature body; threefold entity, nature, and compassion.[b] And:

O child of lineage, this basis abides without impediment as the basis of all [Buddha bodies]—from the viewpoint of entity, the body of attributes; from the viewpoint of nature, the complete enjoyment body; from the viewpoint of compassion, the emanation body. Hence, it is the basally abiding three bodies.[c]

and:

It is beyond[d] the three classes of philosophy. Because it is from the start pure of compounded phenomena, it is spontaneously established, self-arisen pristine wisdom.

And [the *Tantra of Great Luminous Meaning Devoid of*

---

[a] It is youthful in that it does not admit of any degeneration. This mode of subsistence is contained within our bodies; it is contained, or encased, internally and is not showing itself externally now. Thus it is like a statue set inside a pot.

[b] It is set forth extensively with these many synonyms, but they do not pass beyond this encased youthful body.

[c] Because it abides and dwells at all three times, it is the "basally abiding three bodies."

[d] The term *ja log* (7a.5) is to be understood as meaning "reversed from" or "passed beyond."

Proliferation] teaches that places of going astray with respect to the view are eliminated:

> That it is self-arisen eliminates straying into causes and conditions. That it abides empty eliminates straying into effective things. That it is luminous eliminates straying into [mere] emptiness.

And similarly, places of going astray with respect to the eight collections of consciousness are eliminated:[a]

> To indicate the character of the mental consciousness,
> It acts as the overlord of [the sense consciousnesses], partaking of the five external objects.
> The afflicted mentality internally apprehending those
> Is the overlord of the two factors of apprehended-objects and apprehending-subjects.
> Therefore conceptual consciousnesses are the artifice of self-knowledge.[b]
> Apprehensionless luminous basic knowledge itself
> Moves in knowledge but is without the entity of apprehension.
> Though one makes use of external objects, if there is no apprehension,
> The perspective is unhindered vividness, reversed from mentality.[c]

---

[a]   The eight collections of consciousness are the five consciousnesses through the doors of the senses, the mental consciousness, the afflicted mentality, and the mind-basis-of-all.

[b]   Using the example of fire and smoke, smoke is the artifice of fire. Instead of paying attention to fire which is the source, we usually pay attention to its artifice.

[c]   Although these consciousnesses come from basic knowledge, basic knowledge is without the entity of apprehension. Since this

and so forth; this describes how basic knowledge is beyond mentality[a] and the six operative consciousnesses.[b] And:

> If conceptuality does not gather in the seven col-
> lections of consciousness,
> One passes beyond the basis-of-all that is the con-
> necting link.

and so forth, and:

> With respect to the favorable class, through puri-
> fying the eight collections [by viewing them as ba-
> sic knowledge] one passes beyond these.

and:

> The enumeration of the eight collections is as fol-
> lows: the consciousnesses of the five doors [that is,
> the five sense consciousnesses], mental conscious-
> ness, afflicted mentality, and the basis-of-all,
> which is the storehouse accumulating the various
> [seeds]. Those are the phenomena of cyclic exis-
> tence. How do those proceed in cyclic existence?
> Due to not identifying the basis-of-all that is the
> basic reality, through the artifice of basic knowl-
> edge objects are engaged, whereby the eight collec-
> tions of consciousness dawn.

and so forth, and:

> The artifice that is the stirring of basic knowledge

---

basic knowledge has no apprehension, the view of the basic self-knowing knowledge is of unhindered vividness, even though one makes use of external objects.

[a]   The seventh consciousness.

[b]   They are called operative consciousnesses because they oper-
ate on objects.

is stirred by wind; it is called "mentality."[a] From the viewpoint of the function of that mentality, it permeates the eight collections of consciousness.

and so forth. These [passages] speak of:

- how the eight collections dawn from the artifice of basic knowledge;[b]
- and if one does not realize the mode of subsistence of the basic knowledge, the pristine wisdom, one wanders in cyclic existence by means of the eight collections of consciousness;
- and if one realizes pristine wisdom, the eight collections of consciousness dawn as the five pristine wisdoms.

In that way, the consciousnesses of the eight collections, the substrata, are not the ultimate that is being ascertained by the path of the Great Completeness, whereas the noumenon of the minds of the eight collections—basic knowledge and emptiness, fundamental pristine wisdom, self-arisen and uncompounded—is the mind of clear light to be pointed out and recognized.[c] The naturally clear

---

[a]   There are appearances of that basis from that basis; appearances are stirred up by wind. We have to differentiate between two types of wind: one is karmic wind, and the other is wind of pristine mind. Karmic wind cannot have any effect on basic knowledge, which is beyond being affected, beyond cause and effect, and so forth. Thus, the wind being referred to here is the wind of pristine knowledge. Through karmic winds, conceptuality appears as the artifice of the basic knowledge, like the example of smoke and fire; the consciousness that apprehends such conceptuality is called "mentality" (*yid*).

[b]   The eight collections do not dawn from basic knowledge; rather, they dawn from the artifice of basic knowledge.

[c]   The mind of clear light is to be introduced to students

maṇḍala of the mind,[a] the suchness of Secret Mantra, is
this. The path of release [from obstructions], the meaning
of the fourth initiation introduced by way of the lama's
quintessential instructions, is this.[b] The innate factuality
[that is, the fundamental innate mind of clear light] dawning as an imprint of the winds and minds entering the central channel by way of the path of method [such as in the
Guhyasamāja Tantra] is also this.

---

through Great Completeness practices.

[a]   "Mind" here does not mean mistaken mind; the reality of all
phenomena is contained within this mind.

[b]   The path of the union of method and wisdom causes the
karmic winds to enter into the central channel, thereby causing
the winds of pristine wisdom to become manifest from within,
by oneself. It is the innate pristine wisdom that is to be introduced and recognized at the point of the fourth initiation, the
highest initiation. It is what is to be actualized.

2. Uncompounded Wisdom

Those who understand as the actual pristine wisdom something that is a new putting together of (1) a momentary compounded mind and (2) an uncompounded mere emptiness make evident their own internal poverty of not having identified basic knowledge due to not having a lama's quintessential instructions. From the perspective of all those who have not been introduced to the entity of actual innate basic knowledge through a lama's quintessential instructions, it is thought that although emptiness is uncompounded, how could it be possible for what is luminous, knowing, and blissful to be anything other than compounded? That they think this only arises due to the force of not having realized the unified mode of subsistence.

Here, with respect to "luminous and knowing,"[112] if this involves apprehension in the context of having marks, then indeed it would be suitable for it to be compounded. However, although [basic knowledge] is expressed in words as "empty and luminous,"[113] not even a speck of a mark of those two being different is observed, due to which essentially pure basic knowledge—impartial and signless—has nothing about it that serves as a reason for calling it "compounded."

When such a union is not identified, and persons hear "luminous," nothing other than something compounded dawns to their mind, and when they hear "empty," nothing other than a non-thing dawns to their mind.[a] When

---

[a]   When it is said that it is luminous, nothing appears to that person's mind except that it is compounded; when it is said that it is empty, nothing dawns to such a person's mind except that it is uncompounded. The two get separated. Thus, when union is

they hear "union," they do not understand that these are of one taste; rather, all that they understand is a mere collection together of a thing and a non-thing.

Due to this, they apprehend suchness to be just a mere emptiness, a non-thing, and they understand the knower of that suchness to be a compounded awareness. When they set forth the emptiness of the sūtra system, that is what they describe, and even when they explain the innate [wisdom] of the Mantra system, they cannot draw out even a speck of anything more developed beyond what was explained before, except for just different techniques of paths. Even until the final point of their deaths, they remain without being able to generate any understanding concerning how suchness is beyond the extremes of things and non-things, this being evident in their own treatises.[a]

However, when basic knowledge is introduced and identified as it is, it is decided in evident experience that it is uncompounded. The *Tantra of Great Luminous Meaning Devoid of Proliferation* says:

> The body of attributes, self-arisen basic knowledge,
> Is not established as the entity of anything.
> Hence any doubt that it is a compounded thing with marks is eliminated.

and:

---

mentioned, they do not recognize that luminosity and emptiness are of one taste, and understand nothing other than a mere coming together of something that is compounded and something that is uncompounded.

[a]   That they cannot generate even a verbal understanding of something beyond that can be understood when one looks into their texts.

> In the body of attributes, self-arisen pristine wis-
>   dom,
> There are no causes and conditions and hence
>   nothing compounded.

This is called noumenal fundamental mind.[114] From the
viewpoint of being self-luminous, it is indicated with the
name "mind" or "knowledge." However, it is not a mind
included within the eight collections of consciousness that
are compounded phenomena. The *Tantra Containing the
Definitive Meaning of the Great Completeness* says:[115]

> Self-arisen body without earlier and later
> Is not arisen from mind—it is buddha.
> Due to being immutable, it is devoid of suffering.

and:

> You who are the essence of retinues, listen!
> With respect to the definitive meaning, the dis-
>   tinctive buddha,
> Since there is no basis-of-all, there is no appear-
>   ance.
> Hence, this basal mindless knowledge
> Is not arisen from mind—it is buddha—
> The supreme from among the doctrines of the
>   nine vehicles.

and:

> Because of being without the eight collections of
>   consciousness, it is devoid of mind,
> The self-arisen matrix, the body of attributes.

Since within that mode of subsistence of the undifferentiable sphere [of emptiness] and basic knowledge—known
individually by oneself—there is no mutable mind holding
the various predispositions [from actions], how could this
basic knowledge be the mind-basis-of-all?

Since it is absent the external objects of the six collections of consciousness and absent awareness apprehending the internal self or even a little bit of the marks of their objects, how could it be the consciousnesses of the five doors of the senses, the mental consciousness, or the afflicted mentality?

While, like space, it is without any of the phenomena of effective things or marks—such external and internal marks are not observed—it is empty, unhindered,[116] self-luminous, and seen directly. Although it is such, in this entity of luminosity and knowledge there primordially does not exist even a particle of an aspect of marks, which would be what one was aiming at [in conceptuality]. It is not imputable as having arisen from any causes and as having been produced from any conditions; therefore, it is self-arisen great primordial emptiness, self-luminous, and hence self-arisen pristine wisdom.[117] It is noumenal mind or pristine wisdom of clear light.[118]

Although those who do not have quintessential instructions do not believe in this, it is not that there is no such noumenal knowledge. [For it is taught] not just in Mantra but also in the common vehicle; Maitreya's *Ornament for the Great Vehicle Sūtras* says:[119]

> It is said that aside from the noumenal mind
> Any other mind has a nature that is not clear
>   light.[a]

and Maitreya's *Sublime Continuum of the Great Vehicle* says:[120]

> The clear light nature of the mind

---

[a]   Minds that are other than the noumenal mind are not the clear light that is the fruit of having practiced, but are expressed as having a nature of emptiness.

Is immutable, like space.[a]

The "matrix-of-one-gone-to-bliss" also refers to this mind of clear light.

The *Tantra Containing the Definitive Meaning of the Great Completeness* says:[121]

> Because mistaken mind involves the three times
>   [past, present, and future],
> There comes to be earlier, later, and present in
>   one's life.
> Because the mind has mutability, the body has
>   birth and death.
> Because the varieties of sickness, pleasure, and
>   pain are one's own mind,
> It ripens as cyclic existence.
> Therefore mind is not buddha.

and:

> Because the causes [of mind] are compounded and
>   impermanent,
> They can be destroyed by antidotes, and hence
>   [mind] proceeds according to causation.
> Therefore the immutable self-arisen body of at-
>   tributes
> That is not produced by conditions
> Is the matrix of all phenomena.

---

[a]   Whereas Maitreya's *Ornament for the Great Vehicle Sūtras* speaks of these mistaken minds—that is, minds other than the noumenal mind—as not being the clear light of truth, his *Sublime Continuum of the Great Vehicle* says that the mistaken mind transforms into the manifested state of the nature of the mind. His descriptions appear to be contradictory but are not: the first emphasizes the empty nature of the mind, while the second emphasizes the clear light nature of the mind, which is manifested as a fruit of the path.

and:

> The self-arisen matrix which is the body of attri-
>   butes
> Is the self-arisen body not arisen from causes;
> Fruit not appropriated by conditions;
> Empty basic knowledge, not produced by causes;
> Self-luminous, not produced by causes.
> Pristine wisdom with unhindered vividness, not
>   produced by causes.
> Hence the noumenon, the permanent body,
> Self-arisen pristine wisdom, is not produced by
>   causes.
> Conditionless, it is uninterruptedly self-luminous,
> Not affected by conditions that are antidotes.

and so forth, and:

> Because the matrix of phenomena, the self-arisen
>   body,
> Is the root of cyclic existence and of nirvāṇa,[a]
> Buddhas and sentient beings arise from it.
> Therefore, it is the self-arisen basis-of-all.

and:

> This body of attributes that is the self-arisen basic
>   knowledge
> Has no production or cessation in the three times.
> Without going and coming it abides primordially.
> A concordant example is great uncompounded
>   space.

and:

> The factuality of the basis-of-all is compounded.

---

[a]   If one does not understand it, one is sunk in cyclic existence, and if one understands it, one gains nirvāṇa.

It is not without an antidote.[a]
The self-arisen pristine wisdom that is special in-
 sight
Destroys the basis-of-all from the root.

and:

Beclouded persons lacking realization
Say that even the body of attributes itself is mind.
Therefore, they do not understand the meaning
 from the words.[b]
It is rare to understand the definitive meaning just
 from [thinking about] words.
From this the mind does not become buddhafied.[c]

This indicates that without understanding the mode of subsistence, self-arisen pristine wisdom, one does not become buddhafied through mind.

Then, is it that all paths of the nine vehicles—at the end of which one is to become enlightened upon having performed hearing, thinking, and meditating with the mind—are senseless? To indicate that this is not so, it says:

Through searching for imprints an elephant is
 found.
When you search for the fact from the direction of
 the mind, you will find royal self-knowing pristine wisdom.[d]

---

[a]   It is not something that cannot become non-existent due to an antidote.
[b]   Even though they hear the words in their ears, they do not understand their meaning.
[c]   Because the mind is mistaken, it is not enlightened.
[d]   If you search for that from which mistaken mind arises, you will likely find its reality.

When you find it, you separate from apprehending it as mind.
Having become separated from [such] apprehension, you will attain self-arisen mindless body,
Buddha that is not arisen from mind.[a]

This indicates that at the end of the practices of taking the
mind as the path in the eight vehicles,[b] you take pristine
wisdom as the path and, realizing the meaning of the
Great Completeness, become fully buddhafied, and until
you have realized self-arisen pristine wisdom—the basic
knowledge of the Great Completeness—you are not
buddhafied. The *Tantra of the Expanse of the All-Good Pris-*
tine Wisdom: Refined Gold of Great Value says:[122]

This uncompounded nature body,
Nature of the body of attributes,
Unpolluted basic knowledge, not produced
By causes and conditions, immutable, is like
 space.

The *Tantra of the Great Completeness Equal to Space* says:[123]

Just as lotuses [grow from mud, but] are not polluted by mud,
So the entity of the mind of enlightenment, the
 basis,

---

[a]   Since mind is mistaken, what you are to attain is not arisen
from mind; rather, what you will attain is a state of Buddhahood
that is not arisen from mind.

[b]   Being unable to abandon mistaken conventional mind, one
uses that mind itself as the path. The nine vehicles are the three
external vehicles (Hearer, Solitary Realizer, and Bodhisattva vehicles), the three internal vehicles (Action, Performance which is
also called "Both," and Yoga Tantras), and the three secret vehicles (Mahāyoga, Anuyoga, and Atiyoga vehicles), the Great
Completeness being the same as the last.

Is without the stains of apprehended-object and
  apprehending-subject.
Therefore, this self-arisen pristine matrix
Is not made by anyone and is not fabricated.
It is royal self-arisen basic knowledge.
Hence, this uncompounded exalted mind
Is not destroyed by any antidote.
It cannot be left aside or taken up.
A yogi realizing this meaning has buddha-mind
  while in a human body.
In the self-arisen body [the yogi] has pure speech
And immediately [at death] is the all-good Saman-
  tabhadra itself.

and:

The Buddhas of the three times are devoid of
  mind.
Since they are without the eight consciousnesses,
  they are mindless.
The self-arisen matrix, the body of attributes,
Is pristine wisdom not arisen from mind.

Pristine wisdom is not arisen from mind, but is the mode
of subsistence of the mind, the clear light nature. This is to
be understood as similar to how the emptiness that is the
noumenon of all things is the mode of subsistence of all
things, but is not arisen from those things.[a]

The *Tantra of the View of the Great Completeness: The
Complete Depth of Pristine Wisdom* says:[124]

Since this self-arisen matrix that has subsisted primordially

---

[a]   The emptiness that is the mode of subsistence of phenomena depends on things, since things are emptiness' place of dependence, but emptiness does not arise from those things.

Is not arisen from causes and is not produced
from conditions,
There is also conviction that the body of attributes
Not made by any exertion is self-arisen pristine
wisdom.

and the *Tantra of the Great Self-Dawning Basic Knowledge*
says:[125]

This great body of attributes devoid of possibili-
ties of predication
Dwells in all but none realize it.
In it there is no sentience, no mind, and none of
the mistakenness of ignorance.

and:

In basic knowledge devoid of mind,
The appearances of various [phenomena] are
completed instantaneously.[a]

and:

If you know immutable basic knowledge, that is
the fruit of all doctrines.[126]
If you know mindless basic knowledge, that is the
stainlessness of all doctrines.
If you know what ties up[b] basic knowledge, that is
what is to be abandoned through all doctrines.
If you know insentient[c] basic knowledge, that is
the baselessness of all doctrines.

and:

---

[a]   This is like all phenomena melting into space.

[b]   Like the rope that the Tibetan nomads use to tie up the feet
of their animals so that they cannot move.

[c]   That is, without the mental consciousness and so forth.

How could there be any mistake in the immutable
   mind of enlightenment?
The unmistaken mind of enlightenment pervades
   all transmigrating beings.
This matrix of enlightenment pervading all sen-
   tient beings is equal to [that pervading] all
   Buddhas.
This self-knowing lamp, self-illuminating object
   of light,
Dwells in all but is self-secret, revealed by meth-
   ods.
It is the supreme meaning of the thought of all
   Buddhas of the three times,
Abiding equally without fluctuation in all
   Buddhas.[a]

While fundamental knowledge abiding as the basis, self-
arisen pristine wisdom, does not fluctuate from the
noumenon that is without any apprehensions, its self-
effulgence—self-dawning spontaneous appearances and
luminous appearances of marks—manifests from techniques.[b] At that time it is the practice of leap-over to recognize these as the effulgence of the noumenon through
self-arisen wisdom lamps without the apprehended-objects

---

[a]   There are two kinds of secrecy. In the first kind you know
something and keep it hidden from others, but in the other if,
for instance, somebody in a past generation put a treasure under
this house, it would be secret to us, hidden from us, and would
not help us at all. Similar to this latter type, this self-knowing
lamp, this self-illuminating object of light, is with us at all times,
but is secret from us, though right within us now. If someone
identifies it, it is the same as the supreme meaning of the thought
of the Buddhas of the three times.

[b]   The techniques are ways of sitting, ways of gazing, and so
forth that cause these to appear.

and apprehending-subjects of object and subject. Their
basis of dawning is the fundamental mind abiding as the
basis.[a] That previous tantra says:

> The cause of realization is basic knowledge.
> The means of realization is wisdom.

and:

> Mind and predispositions are not the actual bud-
> dha.

---

[a]   When these appearances occur, you are on the level of
knowledge, or wisdom, called "self-arisen lamp." Instead of taking as your objects the external objects of the five senses, you are
beyond that level. Not involved in apprehended-objects and apprehending-subjects, these being the sphere of the five senses and
mind, there are appearances of self-arisen lamps, dawning as the
effulgence, color, or complexion of the noumenon.

The term "leap-over" (*thod rgal*) comes from within the
context of breakthrough and leap-over. "Breakthrough" is recog-
nition of the essential purity that is the nature of phenomena,
and is posited from the viewpoint of emptiness, whereas leap-
over is posited from the viewpoint of spontaneity. The word
"leap-over" is also used occasionally in the sūtra system, and in
general it means that instead of proceeding according to the
stages of the path, one jumps over certain levels. Just as breakthrough is associated with the essential purity which is the emptiness of phenomena, so leap-over is associated with the spontaneous lamps that are beyond object and subject—these appearances being understood as the effulgence, complexion, or color of
the noumenon.

The basis of the dawning of these leap-over factors, the
spontaneous leap-over appearances of the self-arisen lamps, is the
fundamental mind abiding as the basis. In connection with one's
inner channels and so forth, this inner reality lets forth an effulgence that appears out through the eyes, whereby these appearances appear to the eyes.

Pristine wisdom, basic knowledge, is devoid of
  mind and predispositions.

and:

In self-arisen pristine wisdom there are no words,
no letters, no grounds and paths, no mentality, no
mind, no ignorance, no adventitious arisings, no
rising up [of conceptuality], no dormancies, no
aspects, no visionary experience.[a] Therefore, this
[inconceivable reality without any proliferations]
is called the view not limited in its extent and not
fallen to any quarter.[b]

It is thus: pristine wisdom not over-extended
such that it has become ruptured; view not fallen
into any quarter; noumenon pervading all [from
sentient beings up through Buddhas]; unimpeded
wisdom;[c] self-release[127] without apprehension; non-
conceptual self-effulgence; pristine wisdom without having to cease anything;[d] fivefold light without attachment; noumenon in which there is release on that spot itself; spontaneously established
buddha; basic knowledge devoid of mind; buddha
devoid of breath; vivid non-conceptual meditation; lifestyle without grasping and attachment;
view without assertions [of hopes and fears]; fruit
of seeing suchness; [natural, spontaneous]
activities not achievable [through exertion];

---

[a]   There are no various types of visions appearing to the mind.
[b]   It is not permanent, impermanent, and so forth.
[c]   Though it is self-arisen basic knowledge, in the sūtra system
it is identified as wisdom from among the six perfections, unimpeded wisdom.
[d]   When this non-conceptual self-effulgence occurs, it is not
necessary to stop anything.

> pristine wisdom of great self-purification [in which defilements are purified of their own accord].

and:

> Furthermore, mentality does not perceive pristine wisdom, nor make it clearer. In pristine wisdom there is no conceptuality. Because mentality involves the coming and going [of conceptuality], it obstructs the path of Buddhahood.

and:

> Whoever has apprehension
> Does not have self-arisen pristine wisdom.
> When one comes under the influence of meditatively cultivating
> Self-arisen pristine wisdom,
> [All] theses are contradicted from the start.

and:

> If in that way you realize self-arisen pristine wisdom, you are primordially released; it is not necessary [to be released] again. Being self-releasing, there is no [need for] antidotes [to cause release].

Regarding this statement of the mode of arising of the four releases,[a] these do not occur from being introduced to and identifying the minds of the eight collections of

---

[a]   Primordial release and self-release are the first two of four releases. The third is naked release; when conceptuality appears, if you just watch its entity, it is nakedly released. The fourth is dawning release; just as in writing on water, whatever you write immediately disappears, so as conceptuality dawns, it immediately disappears and immediately is released.

consciousness.[a] The *Mirror of the All-Good Exalted Mind Tantra* says:[128]

> If you assert that the basis-of-all is the body of at-
> tributes, you have deviated from me.
> If you assert that Buddhahood is [attained] from
> the mind, you have deviated from me.
> If you assert meditation that has an object, you
> have deviated from me.
> If you adhere to an empty object, you have devi-
> ated from me.
> If you meditate on something other-arisen having
> marks, you have deviated from me.

and so forth.

In brief, in all of the divisions of the Great Completeness—mind-class, expanse-class, and quintessential-
instruction-class—a self-luminous factuality, pristine wisdom beyond mind, is delineated. The fundamental self-
arisen clear light is introduced and identified upon differentiating basis-of-all and body of attributes, mind and
pristine wisdom, mentality and wisdom; hence, no more
than a small number of scriptural passages are cited here.

Because [such differentiation] is vastly well renowned
in the great omniscient [Long-chen-rap-jam's] Seven
Treasuries and so forth, the assertion that the Great Completeness is compounded and is consciousness is very devi-
ant. The former scripture says:

> Whereas all phenomena have the nature of basic
> knowledge,
> Those who see phenomena as mind have deviated
> from you.

---

[a] The minds of the eight collections of consciousness are
mistaken minds—perceiving something that does not exist as
existing—and therefore cannot be a source of release.

The *Great Completeness Lion of the Culmination of Artifice Tantra* says:[129]

> The self-voice of the Great Completeness,
> Is beyond the objects of appearance and emptiness,
> Beyond mind, mentality, and phenomena.

and the *Inlaid Jewels Tantra* says:[130]

> Mind is the root of all predispositions.
> It is indicated as the initial defilement of all sentient beings.
> Mentality, like wind, gathers together the predispositions.
> It is described as the second defilement of sentient beings.
> Breath, like water, is the abode of all predispositions.
> It is the third defilement of all sentient beings.
> The five poisons, like fire, increase appearances with respect to objects.
> It is the fourth defilement of all sentient beings.
> These four thoroughly abide in all transmigrating beings.
> In the body of attributes pure of defilements, how could there be any mental defilements or marks!
> The pristine wisdom body pure of defilements
> Is the mind of enlightenment devoid of actualities of marks;
> Hence the pristine wisdom of basic knowledge is not anything.[a]

and the *Monarch of Multitudinous Expanse Tantra* says:[131]

---

[a]   The pristine wisdom of basic knowledge does not have any of the defilements that were explained above.

Those who view the unproduced noumenon
   within the dualism of causes and conditions
Have turned away from the uncompounded,
Making superimpositions[a] and deprecations re-
   garding the meaning of reality.
They are deceiving themselves—how pathetic it is!

and:

Through being set in its own place just as it is,
The meaning of immutability appears in basic
   knowledge, like space.
Hence in that there is no distraction or non-
   distraction.
No matter what one does, one is within that
   state.[b]

and the *Foremost Powerful Excellent Great Completeness Tantra* says:[132]

Its entity is undemonstrable, uncompounded,

---

[a] Superimpositions are to consider what does not exist to exist, and deprecations are to consider qualities, for instance, that
do exist not to exist. The Tibetan word for superimposition (*sgro
btags*) literally means "adding on feathers"; the shaft of an arrow
without any feathers on it will not go very far; however, if you
put four sets of feathers on it, it will go extremely far. Similarly,
with superimposition once you start adding on to what actually
exists, it just increases greatly.

[b] Because the meaning of immutability appears in basic
knowledge which is like space due to allowing it to be set in its
own place just as it is, in that there is no distraction nor non-
distraction. For a beginner, there can be distraction, but once the
basic mind has manifested itself in fullness, there is no distraction
or non-distraction. No matter what one does, one remains
within that state. No matter what appears, no matter what one
does, it is like the movement of basic reality that is like space.

Beyond words, the matrix, the mind of enlightenment.

and the *All-Creating Monarch* says:[133]

Self-arisen, it arises without causes and conditions,
Pristine wisdom unimpededly luminous.

and:

When my nature is known,
All phenomena are known,
Whereby one is beyond actions and agents, and
achievement through exertion.
[Buddha qualities] are established without exertion.[a]

and:

In this mind of enlightenment, the matrix of all
phenomena,
There is no need to seek and accomplish it with
the ten natures.[b]
As an example of my entire nature it is like space.
In pure space no exertion is to be made.

and:

---

[a]   You might think that if it is beyond all action, agent, and
exertion, and beyond all expression and so forth, then it would
be like nothing, like just space itself, but it is not; it is replete
with good qualities.

[b]   The ten natures are factors such as the five paths and ten
grounds. Because this mind of enlightenment is the fruit state of
pristine wisdom, the qualities of Buddhahood and so forth are
spontaneously established within it; there is no need to seek them
through techniques of paths.

Because I am primordially devoid of apprehended-
      object and apprehending-subject,
I am not designatable in words as "subtle."[a]
I am primordial self-arisen pristine wisdom.
I am not to be ascertained by another [practice].[b]

and:

The scriptures of monkey-like teachers who are
      not valid
Are beset by conceptuality of mistaken teachings
      and paths.
Therefore since masters using a black mineral on
      gold
Are invaluably precious treasures teaching reality,
      they are suitable to be bought.[c]

and:

---

[a] Because there is no basis of designation in this body of attributes of basic knowledge, there is nothing to be imputed as
being subtle.

[b] Since I am the pristine wisdom that is the fundamental reality, when this is manifested, it does not need to be delineated by
any other path.

[c] Proper teachers are like persons who use a black mineral
(*nag mtshur*) that causes the color of gold to come forth in great
brilliance even if it has become befouled and so forth. They are
like precious treasures who teach correctly. Just as when one puts
this black mineral on gold, it makes the gold look even worse but
when one then puts it in fire its color comes out in its full brilliance, so when such a teacher teaches about the Great Completeness, at first the student does not understand much of anything at all, but when implemented in the fire of practice, it
flames forth with all of its brilliance. Since the gold has become
purified, it is of tremendous value, and hence is suitable to be
bought.

Those propounding that there is cause and effect
In the Great Completeness, the highest of all
    yogas,
Are not imbued with the meaning of having real-
    ized the Great Completeness.
When the conventional and the ultimate are pro-
    pounded as dual,
These are words of superimposition and depreca-
    tion.
Realization of them as non-dual is lacking.
Realization of the Buddhas of the three times
Is not seen dualistically, but is asserted as just
    natural placement.

And it says that in comparison with the path of the Great Completeness, in which basic knowledge is directly perceived without exertion, there is little progress through cultivating the stage of completion involving marks of mental apprehension:

If one analyzes those seeking the path of mental
    isolation—
Imputed with the name of a subtle approach—
And keeping solitude in an isolated place,
They are cultivating conceptuality.[a]

---

[a]   In Highest Yoga Tantra, the stage of generation is associated with method and is cultivation of oneself as a deity, whereas the stage of completion is associated with wisdom and is meditation on emptiness. The stages of generation and completion are below the level of Great Completeness of Atiyoga. Thus through cultivating certain levels of the stage of completion that involve marks of holding the mind, or mental apprehension, there is little progress compared to that of the Great Completeness. When you look into these levels of the stage of completion, it really seems that they involve cultivating conceptuality.

and:

> Because the mind of enlightenment is without
>   causes and conditions,
> It cannot be measured within the scope of worldly
>   practices that are produced and cease.
> Because the [ultimate] mind of enlightenment is
>   not produced by conditions,
> It cannot be exemplified with worldly phenomena
>   involving production.

In that way, in the tantras of the Great Completeness—mind-class, expanse-class, and quintessential-instruction-class—mind and basic knowledge are differentiated,[a] whereupon uncompounded pristine wisdom is taken as the path, and factors of compounded consciousness are not taken as the path. Taking the fruit as the self-arisen path without any exertion is the path of Atiyoga.

Aside from just these scriptures [cited above], I will not write down more since it would take too many words, but through merely these it can be understood. Not only is such in the tantras of the Great Completeness, but also the *Compendium of the Thought of the Sūtras* in the doctrinal class of scriptural Anuyoga speaks extensively about the suchness of the mind:

> With respect to delineating the luminous mode of
> subsistence that is the nature of the mind, the
> noumenon of the mind is the self-arisen pristine
> wisdom of Vajrasattva. That pristine wisdom has
> the nature of space since it is without inherent
> existence.

---

[a]   Just as a swan can take a mixture of milk and water and drink out just the milk, without drinking any of the water, so one is to differentiate between mind and basic knowledge.

and:

> Lord of Laṅkā,[a] that which is the suchness of
> [your] mind and that which is the suchness of Va-
> jrasattva are non-dual and not to be taken dualis-
> tically.

and:

> The suchness of Vajrasattva is unfabricated, un-
> polluted, unmade, unanalyzed, and just as it is.
> The suchness of the minds of all sentient beings
> also is unmade, unpolluted, and so on and pri-
> mordially just as it is.[b] O Lord of Laṅkā, those

---

[a] Between the last Buddha, Dīpaṃkara, and the present Buddha, Shākyamuni, there was an intervening period during which
the Mantra teaching started, both the old and the new tantras.
During this time lived the Lord of Laṅkā, a winged monster who
took over the whole world system. Eventually a certain deity entered his body and grew up within his body, causing him excruciating pain. From within this excruciating pain, the monster
asked for help from the Buddhas, saying that he had done many
terrible things, and now [in this quotation] a Buddha is speaking
to him, causing him to identify his own mind.

[b] The nature of the mind is unfabricated (*ma bcos pa*), which
means that it is pure and clear. In a small pool of clear water, you
could see down to all the small stones on the bottom. You might
think that you could see more clearly by stirring it with a stick,
but that would only stir up all the befoulment so that you could
not see anything. Similarly, with the nature of the mind, when
you get some sense of its clarity, and then you think with conceptuality, "This is it," that stirs up your mind such that you
cannot see anything.

Between the Old Translation School and the New Translation Schools there are many controversies, one of which concerns
just this unfabricatedness. Those who refute that we should seek
merely to *manifest* unfabricated mind are thinking in terms of

who wish to gain ascertainment of Secret Mantra
should recognize the suchness of the mind.

and:

The suchness of the mind is the door of purification. It is the door of perceiving the doctrine. It is

---

mistaken mind—that if you leave mistaken mind just as it is
without fabricating anything, without making anything new,
that would be a great fault. But that is not the unfabricatedness
we are talking about here. What we are saying is that you are to
leave the nature of the mind, the noumenon of the mind, as it is,
unfabricated, and once you have differentiated between mistaken
mind and unmistaken mind, you need to leave it unfabricated.
Since the New Translation Schools' refutation is made within
not differentiating mistaken mind and non-mistaken mind, the
refutation does not hit its mark at all.

If the noumenon of the mind, basic knowledge, is exempli-
fied with clear water, to make refutations of others' systems and
establishment of your own position would be like putting the
stick of conceptuality in that water, stirring it up, just making a
mess. They will not let you get down to the fact. When the self-
entity, the own-face, of the Great Completeness is introduced to
a student, a quintessential instruction is to not invite thoughts
about the past or thoughts about the future; rather, set the mind
just in its own nature right in the present. Thus, it is not something to be analyzed by the level of the mistaken mind. It is unpolluted, unmade.

In the first instant, the mind appears as it is, and you are to
leave it as it is, without letting conceptuality get started. If conceptuality gets started, the nature of the mind does not remain,
except for that one moment. It is entirely lost. The minds of all
sentient beings are on the level of superficial mistaken mind that
becomes happy so easily, sad so easily, and the like. But there is a
nature of that mind, an unmoving nature of the mind, and except for the fact that you have not identified it, this nature of the
mind is with you at all times.

the sphere of reality.

and:

The secret sphere is self-knowing.[a] Hence, it is called self-arisen pristine wisdom.

and so forth. The root of all phenomena is the mind of enlightenment.

The excellent quintessential instruction, the great
    method with little difficulty,
Of immeasurable meaning, easy to do, difficult to
    fathom,

and:

Therefore, the thought of the excellent ones
Is contained in that ultimate, unfabricated basic
    mind.
The nature of the mind is unmade and self-arisen.
Hence it is "meditative stabilization" devoid of all
    objects of observation.
In that mind of enlightenment ascertained thus
There are no places to be progressed to[b] and no
    object to be viewed.

---

[a]   With respect to the word "sphere" (*dbyings*), there are the external sphere, the internal sphere, and the secret sphere. Some identify the external sphere as space, which lacks obstructive contact, but I think that the meaning should be associated with practice, and thus I take it to be a sphere appearing to a meditator in which there are various appearances, like honeycombs or little boxes. The internal sphere is that very same ground of appearance in which various things like vajra chains and so forth appear. The secret sphere is self-knowing basic knowledge, which, when manifested, makes one a Buddha.

[b]   There is no sense of a traveler and something traveled, or someone making progress and that over which progress is made.

Hence, it is devoid of all marks, and disadvantage
and advantage are primordially absent.[a]
It is the completion of the two great collections;
all doubts are annihilated,
Conclusively decided in unsurpassed Great Completeness.[b]

and:

When the all-containing profound secret perspective—
Self-arisen, self-knowing basic knowledge—
appears vividly in direct perception,
This is called "self-arisen pristine wisdom seeing
suchness."
When in that way the excellent perspective is seen,
The darkness of ignorance of the collections of
conceptuality is cleared away, being beyond objects seen,
Set [in inconceivable reality] with nothing to be
done, no perception, no seeking.

and:

The factuality of all phenomena, illuminating self-
arisen self-knowing pristine wisdom,
Is unarisen, not produced, and will not be produced,
Primordially devoid of anything to be designated
as cause and effect.
Those who know it in this way complete the two
collections of merit and wisdom.

---

[a]   There is no place for hope and no place for fear.
[b]   Everything is decided, come to completion in the Great
Completeness than which there is none higher. In the three top
vehicles—Mahāyoga, Anuyoga, and Atiyoga—it is Atiyoga.

And the *General Tantra of the Great Lotus Sovereign Gone to Bliss* says:[134]

> When the phenomena of cyclic existence of thor-
>   ough affliction
> Are purified, there is nirvāṇa.
> The root is contained in the noumenon of the
>   mind.
> Through abiding well in great enlightenment,
> The unmade, unfabricated, spontaneous
> Clear light nature of the mind,
> One becomes devoid of all activities involving ex-
>   ertion.
> Just as basic mind having clear light as its nature
> Is naturally unfabricated,
> In this all-encompassing great clear light
> Basic mind—wish-granting jewel—
> Abides without exception in all sentient beings
> Of the three realms, but is not seen,
> Like butter within milk.
> Those skilled in these two draws out the butter.[a]

The *Miraculous Secret Essence*[135] also similarly delineates the nature of the mind with "The foundationless basic mind" and so forth, and the *Miraculous Transcendence Great Tantra* says:[136]

> The nature of immutable great bliss
> Is not a thing nor a non-thing.
> Nor is it observed even as the mere middle.

---

[a]   When you look at milk, you do not see any butter at all, but the butter is there pervading it. When the milk is churned, the butter manifests. Just as someone who churns butter can get but-ter out of milk, so one who is skilled in these two, that is to say, method and wisdom, is able to draw out the butter of manifest-ing the mind of clear light.

Great bliss is described as the great seal.[137]

and the *Guhyasamāja* says:[138]

> The non-existence of a self of phenomena
> Is equal with regard to cognitions of self and ag-
> gregates;
> Hence, one's own mind is from the start non-
> produced
> And has the character of emptiness.

and the *Hevajra* says:[139]

> This meditative stabilization is very subtle
> Like the center of vajra space.[a]

and:

> In this there is no beginning, middle, or end.
> There is no cyclic existence and no nirvāṇa
> There is nothing other than the selfless.
> This is the supreme great bliss.

In brief, the *Mad Elephant Tantra* says:[140]

> Obeisance forever to the equal mind of enlight-
> enment—
> The nature of the mind being the great sky of the
> sphere of reality,
> Phenomena being pure primordially clear light—
> The sphere embedded in natural meaning beyond
> proposition and thought.[b]

---

[a] Like a vajra, it is unbreakable and cannot be overcome. Like the sphere of space, it cannot be said to be this or that.

[b] What is the nature of the mind like? It is unidentifiable. It is the sphere of reality, like great space. Phenomena from forms through to omniscient consciousnesses are naturally pure, and hence are primordially clear light. Yoga realizing this is the sphere of that which has arrived at this natural meaning and is

When such is ascertained, that is the unmistaken, the correct path of the Great Completeness.

---

beyond propositions and faults. Obeisance forever to the mind of enlightenment that is the equal mode of subsistence of all phenomena!

3. Refuting a Contrary View

Nowadays, Ja-ba Do-ñgak[a] claims that the basic mind of the Great Completeness that is to be introduced is a subtle mind.[b] He does this clutching on to others' claims that the so-called "fundamental mind"—at the point of the clear light when meditatively cultivating mental isolation from among the five stages of Guhyasamāja according to the Ge-luk-ba faction—is a subtle mind. Since that subtle mind is a compounded phenomenon produced from four conditions, the Great Completeness would be compounded. There are also some who, following him, repeat this.

This is extremely unsuitable. In general, fundamental mind is the luminous uncompounded nature of the mind, whereby the matrix-of-one-gone-to-bliss also is the same. Holding it to be a compounded mind is indeed a terrible error, but if there is some advantage to describing the clear light of the completion stage of the Guhyasamāja system as compounded, then let those people do as they like. I have

---

[a] Ja-ba Do-ñgak (*ja' pa mdo sngags*), known also as Ja-ba Ngel-wa A-lak (*ja' pa ngal ba a lag*) and Ja-ba drül-gu (*ja' pa sprul sku*), was a fellow student with Mi-pam-gya-tso when both were students of Ba-drül Rin-bo-chay. (For the story of their debate, see pp. 23ff. above.)

[b] Ja-ba Do-ñgak had studied the Ge-luk view and had mixed this into the Ñying-ma view, whereas they differ in certain respects. Specifically, Ge-luk identifies the clear light—a subtle mind that manifests in the cultivation of mental isolation from among the five stages of Guhyasamāja—as being fundamental mind. Taking his lead from that, in his book on the basis, path, and fruit of the Great Completeness Ja-ba Do-ñgak says that the basic mind of the Great Completeness that is to be introduced to practitioners is such a subtle mind.

no wish to refute them, but there is no sense at all in mixing that with the Great Completeness. The description of the Great Completeness as a compounded subtle mind, far from helping the teaching of the Great Completeness, scars the teaching greatly. It contravenes the introduction and identification of basic mind as the noumenal uncompounded union of luminosity and emptiness, widely renowned down to the present day in all the doctrines of the Great Completeness—tantras, oral transmissions, and quintessential instructions—and in the statements by the great omniscient Long-chen-rap-jam as well as the lineaged series of the lamas of the Word Transmission and the Hidden Treasure Transmission.[a]

Indeed, the Great Completeness cannot be harmed by those who say that it is not Dharma, but when a mode of the path is set up saying that the Great Completeness is a compounded phenomenon, it is possible that due to the bad era some persons nowadays will repeat these very unsuitable proclamations by those of small intelligence who have not identified basic knowledge, have not realized the essentials of the tantras and oral transmissions, and like to run after whatever others say.[b] This is because in general

---

[a]   All Ñying-ma doctrines are included within two classes: the Word (the famous Ñying-ma tantras and so forth that were brought from India to Tibet by the Indian paṇḍitas and were translated into Tibetan by them) and the Hidden Treasure (texts later revealed from under the ground). Concerning the latter, Padmasambhava determined the types of quintessential instructions that would be needed in the future and put texts into the ground to be revealed later by his own incarnations.

[b]   When the Great Completeness is refuted by whosoever says that it is not Dharma, they cannot harm it, but when people set up a system saying that the Great Completeness is a compounded phenomenon, they really hurt the teaching. Persons nowadays do not identify the basic knowledge, and they do not

some even take up what is said in the bad systems of the [non-Buddhist] Forders; Dharmakīrti's *Commentary on (Dignāga's) "Compilation of Prime Cognition"* says:

> There are those who repeat even what is said in
> these [non-Buddhist texts].
> Thereby awful darkness is spread about.

And in particular, in this bad era there are many cases of types of dark-side demons who, contemptuous of the teaching, [enter inside people and] divert their minds such that they generate hesitation with respect to the doctrine.

In particular, profound and decidedly secret doctrines are very difficult to understand, due to which it is not suitable to just propound whatever comes to mind. In this way, the *Compendium of the Thought of the Sūtras* says:

> Their minds have not become proficient
> In the secret essence, the intended meaning,
> And yet they make effort at propounding it.
> If they did not speak about it, would it not be better?

> Likewise, those who possess [improper] lifestyles
> And who make proofs and perform analysis,
> What would be wrong if they held back
> Until gaining a mind ascertaining the meaning?

and:

> In future eras their fabricated, perverse, secret[a]
> words

---

realize the essentials of the tantras and the oral transmission of quintessential instructions. Due to this terrible time in which we live, it is possible that such people will repeat the unsuitable proclamations of small minds.

[a]   They use vocabulary that other people cannot make out.

> Will disturb the stainless secret teachings;
> The Word will become polluted and proper texts
>   discarded,
> Making senseless wrong doctrines widespread.

and:

> Just as the blind who have set out on a path
> And try to measure their steps mentally
> Rush to a path bringing terrible fright,
> So these are making estimates from mere guesses.

Accordingly, the *Quintessence of the View of the Great Completeness: The Broad Expanse of Space Tantra*[141] says that this is the situation of those fancying themselves to be wise who have heard a great deal about textual systems and have generated scattered experience within the context of making use of the mind but have not identified basic knowledge through quintessential instructions of the ear-transmission:

> Although the profound meaning of the birthless
>   Great Completeness is profound,
> There are those who, due to not having realized it,
>   make a lot of criticisms.
> Just as it is difficult to find a precious jewel,
> So bad humans in the future
> Will be plentiful and, having quick dispositions,
>   will from sudden feelings
> Not believe the meaning of the Word.
> Criticizing the terms of many texts, they will fo-
>   ment conceptions.
> Rather than enlightenment, they will achieve
>   profit and fame.
> Due to being very lazy, signs of actual achieve-
>   ment will be very distant.

Anxious to enter into practice, they will be quick
to give it up.

They will take on the great burden of finding con-
tradictions in the definitive meaning,

Making superimpositions and deprecations with
regard to words of truth,

Making fine distinctions in words but rough
about the meaning.

Prone to being satisfied with hearing and thinking,

Having understood [a little], they will not put it
into practice and will neglect it.

They will confuse and mix higher and lower texts,

Intent on doctrines made up by humans that are
not the Word.

Merchandising the profound quintessential instructions,

Unwilling to work hard at quintessential instructions having few words

But having profundity taking one to the depths,
they will get angry, saying that these are opaque.

Not allowing instructive advice to penetrate their
minds,

They will not believe in what brings about realization of suchness,

And therefore set up reasoning [for the sake of
criticism].

Though they will lecture a lot, it will be senseless.

People will speak of their good qualities, saying
they are wise.

About persons who deride lamas

They will say, "They are right," and follow them.

Not understanding secret quintessential instructions

They will not act properly as students, and so
   teachers will get fed up.
Not valuing quintessential instructions
From authentic sources as unerring,
They will believe and hold to be holy
What has been mixed with self-fabrications,
Flattering those of low views.
At such a [pathetic] time,
In just that moment when they start teaching doc-
   trine,
Buddhas endowed with tantras and oral teachings
   will become concerned and fearful,
And Hearer sūtra followers will outright faint.
Groups of gods, demi-gods, and monsters will
   bring about interruptions
To the lives of those persons making superimposi-
   tions and deprecations,
Who will completely fall into great hells,
Undergoing various frights there
With their heads and bodies split into thousands
   of pieces.
Those who hold the knowledge will forsake them.[a]
Therefore, it will be difficult to find a student
   who is a suitable vessel
For these very secret meanings.

and:

The teaching of the Great Completeness with
   quintessential instructions has arisen,
And when groups of hypocrites with low view—

---

[a]   Virtuous spiritual guides, seeing that these people are in
such an awful state and are for the time being beyond being
taken care of, will forsake them, since they cannot do anything
for them for the time being.

Forders fancying themselves to be Māntrikas
And those attached to provisional vehicles—
Become angry concerning its explanation of the
definitive view,
They will make derision and nasty criticism.

and so forth, and:

This definitive view of the all-good
Is not hypocritically crafted to curry favor.
Those who without discouragement can explain
this holy doctrine,
Unhesitating supreme of heroes,
Will be blessed by Ones-Gone-to-Bliss
To teach fearlessly, without mistake.
What need is there to mention that the sky-
travelers and doctrine-protectors will do so too?
They will not be affected by sources of harm, and
their merit will increase.

and so forth, and the *Tantra of the Great Completeness
Equal to Space* says:

If you do not possess quintessential instructions
transmitted in the ear,
No matter how much you analyze with your own
analytical mind,
You will not realize this profound transmission.
Due to being without the instructive advice of the
definitive transmission,
A master without the ear transmission
Does not have the definitive meaning,
Whereby an attempt to save another will be for
both a cause to fall.[a]

---

[a]   Just as when someone who is swept away by the current of a
river tries to help somebody else in the same situation, both of

Also, there are many stories of the unfortunate who be-
haved according to the literal words and were reborn in
bad transmigrations.[a] And [the *Tantra of the Great
Completeness Equal to Space* also says]:

> With respect to the self-luminous, non-dual pris-
> tine wisdom,
> They make distinctions of "is" and "is not"
> Due to its not according with their own concep-
> tuality

---

them are drowned, so here when such a person teaches, it only
makes causes of downfall for both teacher and student.

[a]   The unfortunate here are those who take non-literal terms
literally and thus make trouble for themselves. You have to make
a distinction between what is literal and what is non-literal. The
definitive is literal, and the non-definitive is to be taken non-
literally. Consider Buddha's teaching in the *Compilations of Indicative Verse* (XXIX.22 and XXX.73 in Gareth Sparham, *The
Tibetan Dhammapada*):

> Those without ill deeds who, having killed father and
> mother, destroy the monarch, the two cleanly ones, and
> the area as well as the retinue are the pure.

That father and mother are to be killed should be taken non-
literally as meaning that one should eliminate attachment and
grasping. That the monarch should be destroyed should be taken
non-literally as referring to overcoming consciousness that arises
due to the condition of contaminated actions [in the twelve links
of dependent-arising]. That the two cleanly ones should be destroyed should be taken as overcoming holding wrong views to
be supreme and holding modes of conduct to be supreme. De-
stroying the area and retinue should be taken non-literally as
overcoming the objects of afflictive emotions and the twenty
secondary afflictive emotions. Through doing this, one will become pure, that is to say, will gain enlightenment endowed with
the two types of purity—natural purity and purity from adventitious defilements.

And only serve to increase controversy.[a]

[This precious teaching] cannot be darkened by
   other [outside forces]

But just as a lion is destroyed [by a worm] inside
   its gut,

So this secret transmission is made to vanish

By those asserting that they are my children.[b]

How will this happen?

and so forth, and:

Although they meditate on the clear light basic
   mind

With mistaken worldly consciousness,

They will not succeed, and their lives will be cut
   short.

and the *Tantra of Quintessential Instructions of the Precious
Lamp of Secret Pristine Wisdom* says:[142]

Wrong tenets are demons to the doctrine.

They make apprehensions of inherent existence in
   that which has none;

They seek for cause and effect in what is just self-
   arisen;

---

[a] Although pristine wisdom is beyond the positions of "is"
and "is not," they hold on to these factors of "is" and "is not"
with respect to it, due to the fact that it does not accord with
their own conceptuality, and through holding on to these proliferations with respect to that which is devoid of proliferations,
they just serve to increase controversy.

[b] A lion, being the king of beasts, cannot be killed by any
other animal, but is destroyed by a worm generated inside its gut
that then destroys the lion from within. Similarly, this secret
transmission of the Great Completeness cannot be destroyed
from the outside, but will be made to vanish by misinterpretation
from within.

Concerning what is unfabricated and is not anything
They analyze with thoughts holding on to this and
that;
Concerning the spontaneously established effect
not involving any progression
They pollute the non-progressive with the pro-
gressions of the eight paths.[a]
Therefore, since no matter how much they analyze
with a mind
Holding on to wrong ideas about the unfabricated
actuality, it is not so.
It is understood by setting in the natural state
without analysis.[b]

and so forth. In these ways, this awful talk of a tenet saying
the Great Completeness is compounded has arisen.[c]

My lama, the holy presence Jam-ȳang-kyen-dzay-
wang-bo,[143] said that the single phrase that the Great Completeness is compounded contradicts all of the essentials of
basis, path, and fruit of the Great Completeness.[d] As
illustrated by that, it displeases the minds of the holy, but
nowadays since we are at an end point [of the doctrine] in
which mere reflections of the teaching are considered to be

---

[a]   These are the first eight of the nine vehicles, which, while
not the final vehicle, are mistaken for being final.

[b]   Allow the clear water of the mind to remain clear without
stirring it up.

[c]   When Mi-pam-gya-tso wrote this, the book by Ja-ba Do-
ñgak had already been burned at Ba-drül O-gyen-jik-me-chö-ḡyi-
ẇang-bo's command.

[d]   Mi-pam mainly heard Śa-ḡya teachings from Jam-ȳang-
kyen-dzay-wang-bo, Ḡa-gyu teachings from Jam-gön-ḡong-drül
Lo-drö-ta-ye, and the Great Completeness from Ba-drül
O-gyen-jik-me-chö-ḡyi-ẇang-bo.

doctrine, there are those who know how to say all sorts of things without even making the slightest analysis as to whether these accord or not with the essentials of Ñying-ma doctrine. This shows signs that the teaching at the heart of Samantabhadra will not remain for a long time— it is very sad.[a]

The Great Completeness is the pristine wisdom of knowledge and emptiness, the meaning to be realized in the fourth initiation.[b] It is that which is to introduced and identified; it is the path to be delineated, and hence is the basis of analysis as to whether it is compounded or un-compounded. This is the noumenon of the mind, self-arisen pristine wisdom. It is not different from the sphere of reality, and since the sphere of reality is self-luminous, it is the mode of subsistence that has primor-dially abided as the noumenon of the mind; therefore, it is the great uncompounded union. In terms of this mode of

---

[a] The body of attributes, Samantabhadra, is a huge Buddha called "Immense Ocean Sage" (*thub pa gangs chen mtsho*) with a bowl of fragrant water resting on his hands that are in the pos-ture of meditative equipoise. A lotus with twenty-five levels of petals on its stalk grows up from the bowl, and our world system, Jambudvīpa, is on the lotus petal right at the level of his heart. A thousand Buddhas will appear in this auspicious era in Jam-budvīpa. The current critical situation is similar to when during a war you have been worn down to the point where there are only a few of you left, and you feel there is just little that can be done, since you are at a time of such ruination. There are very few peo-ple capable of thinking, capable of appreciating the profound meaning, and there are so many people engaged in all sorts of fault-finding.

[b] The four initiations are the vase initiation, the secret initia-tion, the knowledge wisdom initiation, and the precious fourth initiation of the word, in which the Great Completeness is to be identified.

subsistence, all of the phenomena of the three times—past, present, and future—do not pass beyond this immutable equality, due to which it is to be understood as without the proliferations of the three times and of dualistic phenomena.

A compounded and momentary consciousness is not the mode of subsistence of all phenomena. Through identifying it how could suchness be realized? Therefore, since the pristine wisdom of basic knowledge and emptiness that is the Great Completeness is the fundamental, unchanging, and immutable clear light, it is to be comprehended from the side of its being the mode of subsistence. No tantra of the Great Completeness and no lineaged lama—Knowledge-Bearers[144] such as Ga-rap-dor-je[145] and so forth—has taught a compounded mode of subsistence. The awful proclamation that the Great Completeness is compounded is fit for laughter, not fit to be heard.

When yogis who have properly been introduced to and have identified basic knowledge are set in meditative equipoise within the fundamental noumenon, they realize it without even any of the consciousnesses of the eight collections wavering from this state. There, objects to be realized and realizers do not exist as different.[a] If it were the case that a subtle mind were fundamental mind, it would have to be primordial, original basal clear light because of being the fundamental noumenon without the changeability and mutability of the three times. And if it is, it is said that at that time of the primordial, original, basal clear light "there are no Buddhas and no sentient beings," and it is said that in that mere basis there is no mistake, and there is not even any imputation of release

---

[a]   Just as the planets and stars dissolve into the sky in the light of the bright sun, so objects realized and means of realization all become of one taste in the great reality.

from the viewpoint of the reversal of error. Hence, if there is a subtle mind [in that state], why would it not be a sentient being, as is the case with a sentient being of the formless absorptions or a sentient being of no discrimination.[a] Consequently, it would have to be asserted that there is mistake in that state, and no release.

At that time of [realizing] the primordial original reality, does that subtle mind have apprehension of "I" and have apprehension of duality, or not? If it does, then it is a mind of cyclic existence associated with obstructions. How could it be a mind of clear light devoid of obstruction?[b] If obstructions exist in the fundamental mind, the basic disposition,[c] then fundamental mind would be included within cyclic existence and would not be included within nirvāṇa. In that case, this would contradict all of the many scriptures, cited earlier, speaking of the clear light nature of the mind, and so forth.

Therefore, fundamental mind is the noumenon, emptiness, and from the viewpoint of not being a mere emptiness of inherent existence and of not being just an emptiness of matter, it is called "mind of clear light" and "self-arisen pristine wisdom." Aside from only being self-luminous emptiness, it is without even a particle of any marks of being compounded or uncompounded.

---

[a] Although in the Form Realm there are no coarser consciousnesses, there is a subtler type of consciousness, and thus there are sentient beings, as is the case with sentient beings in that level of cyclic existence called "no discrimination," in which the coarser levels of consciousness have disappeared, but there is a subtler type of consciousness, and thus there is a sentient being.

[b] How could it be the basic fundamental mind of clear light of the time of the fruit?

[c] "Fundamental mind" has the same meaning as the fundamental disposition, or mode of subsistence.

Consequently, it is beyond atomically established matter and is beyond luminous and cognitive consciousness having factors of apprehended-object and apprehending-subject. It is to be realized by one's own individual knowledge perceiving suchness, not comparable in the least with any of the consciousnesses of the eight collections.

In that noumenal union of basic knowledge[a] and emptiness there are utterly and primordially no conceptual and constructed apprehended-objects and apprehending-subjects,[146] whereby within natural flow one abides in the non-conceptual sameness of all phenomena. Hence, in it there are primordially no marks[147] of dualistic phenomena—cyclic existence and nirvāṇa, mistake and release, self and other, beginning and end, and so forth. This is the suchness of mind described in the *Hevajra Tantra* and in Virūpa's[b] *Utterly Without Proliferation*[148] as, "This has no beginning, middle, or end," and so forth.

From within the state of such a noumenon there is not at all any fluctuation, but then appearances of conceptuality, appearances of the artifice of the noumenon, dawn upon association with adventitious karmic winds, at which time mind having dualistic appearances operates, and there is apprehension of I-self. Thereupon, the arising of the eight collections of consciousness is called "mind." Due to conceiving [of object and subject] as actualities, the cyclic existence of mistaken dualistic appearance in which the fundamental suchness is not realized arises, and one roams downwards in the process of dependent-arising.[c]

---

[a]   Basic knowledge is that which, when known, one is a Buddha, and when not known, one is in cyclic existence

[b]   Virūpa was an Indian master who was one of the great sources and translators of the Śa-ġya School.

[c]   From ignorance comes action, and so on through the twelve links of dependent-arising.

When one perceives the fundamental meaning, the unmistaken path of the Great Vehicle,[a] the noumenon is realized, whereupon predispositions for mistaken dualistic appearance are extinguished,[b] this being called "buddha." Therefore, the fundamental noumenon, the dispositional mode of subsistence abiding without the changeability and mutability of the three times is taught by way of synonyms such as fundamental mind, mind of clear light, mind of enlightenment, sphere of reality, self-arisen pristine wisdom abiding as the basis, innate great bliss, noumenal suchness, and so forth.

In the minds of all sentient beings such exists in the manner of the noumenon, and during states in which obstructions remain fit to be abandoned [but are not yet abandoned], it is called the "matrix-of-one-gone-to-bliss," because through realizing this noumenon of the mind one is buddhafied. In the same way, you should also understand the mode of designating it as fundamental mind and so forth. In the Kālachakra system, "non-stupid emptiness" has the sense of luminous pristine wisdom that is not a mere emptiness and is without any coming together or separating apart. It is beyond the poles of the compounded and the uncompounded. The suchness of things is not apprehendable as an emptiness devoid of clear light, nor apprehendable as a mind of clear light devoid of emptiness.

When those two [clear light and emptiness] are realized as objects of your own individual knowledge realizing suchness, they are realized to be undifferentiable. When

---

[a]   Within the Great Vehicle, the reference here is to the path of Secret Mantra, and within that, it is to the path of the Great Completeness.

[b]   This extinguishment of predispositions is like the extinguishing of a butter-lamp upon the consumption of its oil.

this is not realized, a mere object of understanding—
wherein from the point of view of conceptual isolates there
is an object, emptiness, which is a mere elimination of an
object of negation and there is a consciousness, an object-
possessor, having marks—may dawn to your mind. However, this does not pass beyond objects of conceptual dualistic consciousness apprehending phenomena with marks,
that is to say, as things and non-things; hence, it is not the
ultimate.

When fundamental mind, suchness, is actualized, this
is the non-dualistic noumenon, known by individual self-
knowledge, passed beyond all dualistic phenomena, such
as thing and non-thing, emptiness and non-emptiness, and
so forth. Consequently, making dualistic divisions within
that, such as emptiness and clear light, or basic knowledge
and emptiness, or appearance and emptiness, and so forth,
are just cases of subsequent conceptuality *expressing* the
mode of not abiding in any partial extremes.[a] In the entity
of suchness there is no duality; it similarly is beyond all
dualistic phenomena of object and subject, and so forth.

This non-dualistic mind of enlightenment is, as was
cited earlier [from the *Mad Elephant Tantra,* see p. 97
above], "The nature of the mind being the great sky of the
sphere of reality," and so forth. Aside from being actualized by one endowed with yoga in dependence upon quintessential instruction of method and release, it is not an
object of analysis by logical reasoning.

Hence, conviction in this is suitable to be generated in
those who have decided that their own minds are without
production,[b] whereas those who assert that the uncompounded mere emptiness that is taken to mind by a

---

[a]   Such expressions are used for beginners.

[b]   In those who have made such a decision, belief then devel-
ops from within.

compounded mind is suchness are only children whose judgment has not matured. Since not even a similitude of individual self-knowledge has been generated, nothing other than that can dawn to their minds, whereupon these tenets [made up] by conceptuality deceive childish beings;[a] therefore, you should give up pursuing that direction and, instead, should listen to instructions of the profound lineage, transmitted ear to ear, from the mouth of excellent knowledge-bearing lamas, getting at the tenets of the Great Seal and the Great Completeness.

In brief, since your own mind is primordially without production, it is beyond all proliferations of things and marks and hence is emptiness, but there is no blockage of the effulgence of the basic knowledge.[b] Aside from that, there is no difference between mere emptiness and a mind knowing that emptiness. The basic mind is self-empty, and emptiness is self-luminous. Luminosity and emptiness are undifferentiable and utterly without the conceptuality of apprehended-objects and apprehending-subjects. Such a noumenon that is this way due to its primordial disposition is nominally imputed as "fundamental mind."[c]

It is primordially not established as the two, a mind that is the knower and the emptiness that is the object of knowing. Therefore, it is the great uncompounded union.[d]

---

[a]   Like one child telling stories to another child.

[b]   Our bodies and consciousnesses block up the effulgence of the basic knowledge. We have this basic knowledge within us, but our bodies and consciousnesses block it. Through the three modes of posture and the three modes of viewing in the practice of leap-over, these become unblocked, and it dawns.

[c]   For the sake of causing others to understand it, it is merely designated with the name "fundamental mind."

[d]   Union here means that which is already unified; thus, it is union—a state of already being unified—and is uncompounded,

In the noumenon there are no causes and conditions, no production and cessation; hence, it is uncompounded, but it is not an uncompounded non-actuality.[a]

> In the great clear light of effulgent basic knowl-
>   edge
> Primordially without production from the start,
> There are no continuums of momentary com-
>   pounded things produced and ceasing;
> The three times are just equal.
> It is non-conceptual with no marks of prolifera-
>   tion.
> In that way, in all three times it does not develop
>   and change;
> Hence, it is conventionally designated as funda-
>   mental mind
> Primordially abiding like space.
> Compounded minds, momentarily produced
> And ceasing, are adventitious;
> Hence they are not suitable to be fundamental.
> In consideration of this, even sūtras say
> That consciousness is impermanent and pristine
>   wisdom is permanent.
> About calling fundamental mind "permanent,"
> There is no fluctuation within its own state at any
>   time,
> And hence it is designated permanent.
> Since it is rid of all proliferations of the marks of
>   things,
> The ways of the words "permanent" and "imper-
>   manent"
> Are divisions by dualistic phenomena.

---

and is not some small uncompounded thing and thus is great.

[a]   Unlike space, which is a mere absence of obstructive contact, it is not a mere absence.

When one's own nature devoid of all
Proliferations of marks is comprehended,
One has passed beyond the objects of conceptions
   of permanence and impermanence.
Likewise one has passed beyond all marks of dual-
   istic phenomena—
Thing and non-thing, permanence and annihila-
   tion, and so forth.
Hence, aside from being what is comprehended
By those endowed with yoga realizing
The suchness of mind by themselves individually,
It is not an object of comprehension through the
   dualistic conceptuality
Of examples, reasons, and so forth.[a]
Therefore it is designated with the conventions
Of being devoid of thought and expression
And being beyond awareness and so forth.
Those who realize meaning of this know suchness.

---

[a]   The reference here is to logical syllogisms in which a subject, a predicate, a reason, an example, and so forth are stated.

4. Distinctions

Question: [Within differentiating between basal fundamental mind, path fundamental mind, and fruit fundamental mind,] does basal fundamental mind realize emptiness or not?

Answer: With respect to fundamental mind residing in the basal state [as distinct from when one is on the path or in the fruit state,] there are no conventions of realizing emptiness or not realizing emptiness.[a] [With respect to the mode of subsistence of the basis itself,] its own entity is a clear light emptiness or noumenon, which is a union of basic knowledge and emptiness unpolluted by any conceptuality. Therefore, it itself is suchness and the sphere of reality but not an object to be affixed with the conventions of "realizing" or "not realizing." Realizing emptiness or not realizing emptiness is not posited with respect to the basis itself.[b]

Within the basis abiding as the suchness that is to be realized, appearances of the basis shine forth, whereupon there is realization of the basis as it is, or non-realization, due to which release or mistake come to be. Hence, relative to that, one is designated as a "Buddha" or as a "sentient being."[c]

When the mental consciousness that is the means of

---

[a] Because this question concerns the basic state, fundamental mind is the reality of the mind, and thus all of us have it. Since this is a neutral state, conventions of realizing emptiness or not realizing emptiness do not apply.

[b] These distinctions have to be posited within the context of basal appearances from that basis.

[c] If a person has release, that person is designated as a Buddha, and if a person has error, that person is designated as a sentient being.

realization realizes the fundamental mind abiding as the basis, it is said that "the realizer realizes emptiness."[a] Mistaken sentient beings who have not realized this have the noumenal fundamental mind,[b] but when, being without realization, they have conceptions of marks regarding dualistic appearances of the eight collections of subject-consciousness,[c] this is called "non-realization."

Upon the arising of the array of cyclic existence and nirvāṇa, which are basal appearances as projections from the basis,[d] there are the conventions of the two, mistake and release. In the mere basis, there is nothing that could be designated as mistake or release, Buddha or sentient being, realization or non-realization. The two—cyclic existence and nirvāṇa—are not established in the fundamental mind that is the basis.

Although it is the sole drop[e] that is the great clear light of essential purity, undifferentiable basic knowledge and

---

[a]   At that time, the realizing mind has dissolved completely into fundamental mind, or it can be said that simultaneous with the removal of all defilements with respect to all phenomena ranging from forms up to omniscient consciousnesses, the defilements of that realizing mind are removed.

[b]   Without realizing the fundamental mind they have not recognized their own nature.

[c]   This is how we are bound by conceptions of apprehended-objects and apprehending-subjects.

[d]   The comparison here is like that between fire and smoke: fire is like the fundamental basis, and smoke is like the projective appearances (*rtsal*) from that basis, which are also called effulgence (*gdangs*). Within these projective appearances of cyclic existence and nirvāṇa there come to be the conventions of error and release.

[e]   The sole drop is the single entity that is the mode of subsistence of all phenomena.

emptiness,[a] in which the marks of dualistic phenomena are primordially non-existent, anything and everything are suitable to appear from within the clear light that is the nature,[b] and hence it is called the "basis." Projective appearances dawn, whereupon in the context of those basic appearances there are the two paths of mistake and release,[c] due to which [tantras] speak of "one basis and two paths."[d] Therefore, Long-chen-ba says that projective appearances are the basis of release and [the practice of] essential purity is the ground of release.[e]

Consequently, within the essential purity that is the basis, there is no way of making a differentiation of

---

[a]   The sūtra system speaks of wisdom differentiating phenomena, whereas this tantric system speaks of empty basic knowledge, which is more profound and quicker.

[b]   Like the constellations of the stars and so forth appearing in space, cyclic existence and nirvāṇa are suitable to appear from within the clear light that is the nature.

[c]   When you recognize these projective appearances of the basis as such, there is release, and when you do not, there is mistake.

[d]   There is only one basis for the Buddhas who know and the sentient beings who do not know.

[e]   These projective appearances of the basis are both the basis of mistake and the basis of release through the practice of essential purity, which, therefore, is called the ground of release. Just as the ground of an airport is the place where the people of cyclic existence wander about and also is that from which the plane of those who are released takes off to the heights—the ground of the airport being a single ground for those two activities—so the basic mode of subsistence serves as the basis of both activities of mistake and release. Projective appearances of the basis are the basis of release when you realize them as they are, and they are also the basis of mistake when you do not recognize them properly.

realization and non-realization.[a] In terms of the mode of appearance [of these projective appearances that dawn from the basis], there must be a progression of improvements of abandonments and realizations, ranging from common beings up through Buddhas, and moreover there is nothing fit [to do this] except for these eight collections [of consciousness] in the continuum of the meditator.[b]

In particular, it is taken for granted that the mental consciousness must identify the meaning of [the fourth] initiation.[c] Not only in the Great Completeness, but also in any of the paths of the nine vehicles, all comprehensions by the wisdoms of hearing, thinking, and meditating on any of the paths of the nine vehicles are mainly by the mental consciousness.[d] Hence, there is indeed not anything that is not meditated on by the mind, but it is not that whatever the mind meditates on must be the mind. Even when emptiness is meditated on, it is indeed meditated on by the mind, but emptiness is not mind; it is the object of the mind,[e] and likewise although the Great Completeness

---

[a]   With respect to the ground of an airport itself, you do not say that it flies up in the sky, or that it walks around on the ground.

[b]   There is nothing suitable to do the meditating other than meditating with the meditator's awarenesses of the eight collections of consciousness. There is nothing else suitable for the job. Basic reality is unthinkable and inexpressible—it is not going to be what does the meditating.

[c]   It is basic that it is necessary that the meaning of the fourth initiation be recognized, understood, and identified by the mental consciousness.

[d]   It is the agent of realization.

[e]   It would be extremely absurd to say that whatever the mind meditates on must be mind itself. It is like the fact that although one meditates on emptiness with the mind, emptiness is not the mind, it is the object of the mind.

is meditated on by the mental consciousness, the mental consciousness is meditating on the noumenon of the mind, the union of basic knowledge and emptiness, but this [union] is not the mind that is within the six collections of consciousness.

Just as when the mind meditates on the emptiness that is selflessness, it is not necessary that the mind be or not be emptiness and selflessness, so when the mind is realized as without production or when the mind itself [that is meditating on emptiness] is realized as without production, a mind that is different from the absence of production does not exist even in the slightest,[a] but that absence of production does not become the mind and does not become compounded. [Meditating on the Great Completeness] is similar.

When, in that way, one's own mind is completely decided as without production, that very mind is directly perceived as without production from the start; not even a particle of a factor of mind or consciousness that is other than non-production is observed.[b] Similarly, the entity of the union of luminosity and emptiness, which is the unimpeded self-luminosity of the factor of luminosity and

---

[a]   When the mind realizes the lack of production, that lack of production similarly applies to the mind, and there is not any mind that is left over separate from the absence of production—it, simultaneous with all other phenomena, is seen as just nonproduced.

[b]   When the mind is realized in its basic reality of nonproduction, there is not any mind left over—the mind completely disappears. An example of this is when you see a rope as a snake. When you find out that it is a rope, the mistaken consciousness of it as a snake utterly and completely disappears. There is not any such consciousness left over at all. When the mind is realized as having the basic reality of non-production, there is no mind left over.

knowing of the mind,[a] is called the "noumenon of the mind." From within that noumenon, even all eight collections of consciousness abide as that to be known individually by oneself, a multitude having an equal taste, devoid of verbalization.

Within this, what is there to be identified as a compounded Great Completeness, as "a subtle mind"?[b] There is not any such thing. It should be explained just what sort of system this is that says a subtle mind is the Great Completeness, and that other, coarse minds and so forth—the eight collections of consciousness—are not the Great Completeness.

Not only that, but also from within noumenal fundamental basic knowledge and emptiness, whether cyclic existence or nirvāṇa appears, it appears from within this, and whether one is released, one is released from within this.[c] If this [noumenal fundamental basic knowledge and emptiness] is that which is to be realized in actual experience by yogis of the Great Completeness, then what value is there in identifying and meditating on a momentary subtle

---

[a]   In such an entity of luminosity and emptiness, luminosity is not one thing and emptiness another thing; those two are of one taste. This noumenon, or reality, of the mind is what is to be explained to trainees from beginning to end. It is what is left over when all of the consciousnesses involving apprehended-objects and apprehending-subjects cease.

[b]   A subtle mind would be an impermanent phenomenon, and within that state in which everything is of one taste, how could there be any subtle mind that could be identified as a compounded Great Completeness?

[c]   For all appearances of cyclic existence and nirvāṇa, whatever dawns dawns from within this fundamental basic knowledge and emptiness. When you are released in the path of omniscience, you are released right within the state of this fundamental basic knowledge and emptiness.

factor of mind as the Great Completeness and not the foundation and root of all phenomena, basic mind, the fundamental Great Completeness, fundamental mind?

Therefore, the mental consciousness is the awareness that is the meditator on the Great Completeness. As long as one meditates with that awareness in the manner of the dualistic appearance of apprehended-object and apprehending-subject within observing verbal objects of observation of the path—such as a union of the object, emptiness, and luminosity, and so forth—that is a consciousness having apprehended-object and apprehending-subject and has not even gone in the direction of the Great Completeness, non-dualistic pristine wisdom. However, when you conclusively know in immediacy—like a moist olive in the palm of your hand—your own mind as noumenal empty basic knowledge without object and subject, the convention that the basic knowledge of the Great Completeness has been identified is designated.[a] The process is to be introduced to the basic nature of the mind right within the context of coarse mind and to meditatively get used to this again and again, thereupon coming to decisiveness.[b]

---

[a]   When you manifestly identify the basic nature of mind, not thinking that there is anything beyond what you are seeing, when you come to such decisiveness—like the decisiveness that you have with respect to a moist olive placed in your palm, seeing everything about that olive, both inside and outside, understanding it completely—when you come to such direct decisiveness, without any sense of object and subject with respect to the basic reality of the mind, then it is permissible to designate the convention that Great Completeness basic knowledge has been identified. This is oneself identifying one's own entity, one's own face.

[b]   The lama introduces the student to this basic mind right within the context of a coarse consciousness, and does this again and again, and the student gets used to this again and again,

Just this has been transmitted in quintessential instructions by all of the transmissions of the earlier Knowledge-Bearers, and in all of the fortunate, measures of warmth [that is, signs of success] become manifest.[a] While there still is this uninterrupted transmission of these profound essentials of prescriptive instructions, what is the use of describing a subtle compounded mind, wiping out the doctrinal language of the Great Completeness?

Even the clear light fundamental mind that is described on the occasion of the five stages [in the *Guhyasamaja* system] in terms of melting bliss, mental isolation, and so forth as techniques for realizing it for the sake of those who do not identify it in immediacy is the self-arisen pristine wisdom of noumenal clear light.[b] It is not a subtle mind that is an instance of one of the eight collections of consciousness; such a subtle mind is a momentary compounded factor. Therefore, how could a compounded factor be the noumenon and the mode of subsistence?

Once you have been introduced to and have succeeded

---

attaining decisiveness with respect to the nature of the mind.

[a]   This is the process that has been advised in quintessential instructions, these being easy techniques to bring about success for those who do not know how to meditate.

[b]   For those who cannot identify the basic nature of the mind in immediacy, straight-on in this way, other techniques are explained for realizing it, such as melting bliss, mental isolation, and so forth, these being set forth not only in the New Translation Schools, but also in the Old Translation School. Melting bliss is the ignition of internal fire in order to melt drops of essential fluid and thereby cause the winds to enter into the central channel, inducing deeper states of consciousness. The term "mental isolation" (*sems dben*) refers to a practice in which one's mind becomes isolated from coarser levels of appearance and consciousness and causes them to be pacified, extinguished, dormant.

in identifying the Great Completeness, then although you do not intentionally meditate with exertion on the objects of observation of mental isolation,[a] through familiarizing just with [the Great Completeness], the pure clear light—like unpolluted space—that dawns during thick sleep is manifest. This occurs for those who have previously developed any level of experience with respect to the path of the Great Completeness.[b]

Since there is not any object of realization other than experiencing just this present naked basic knowledge without even a speck of pollution by conceptuality,[c] noumenal self-arisen pristine wisdom dawns. How could this be meditation on the emptiness that is an object understood by a subtle compounded mind left over after stopping the coarse six collections of consciousness? Aside from just abiding in the luminous and empty noumenon[d] without end or middle, how could there be conceptuality that is performing analysis? There is not.

They assert that:

> With regard to delicate clear light[149] and the clear light when meditatively cultivating mental isolation, three appearances dawn in the forward process [before the mind of clear light] and in the

---

[a]   That is to say, even if you do not intentionally try to stop the grosser levels of consciousness.

[b]   During deep dreamless sleep those who have not been introduced to the clear light are unable to actualize the clear light, even though it is there.

[c]   Naked basic knowledge is consciousness of the present moment, in which you do not follow after thoughts of the past, or follow after thoughts of the future, but is just naked present consciousness. At that time, you experience just thus naked present basic knowledge without even the slightest conceptuality.

[d]   It is internally luminous and externally luminous.

reverse process [after the mind of clear light], and there are subtle analyses identifying them.[a] Thinking just of experiencing that mere subtle mind [of mental isolation after the three appearances] without the cessation of the three modes of appearance and analytical identification of them, they assert that the noumenal basal clear light is a subtle compounded mind.

This is like the story of a turtle in a well.[b] How could it be

---

[a]   The three appearances are the white, red, and black appearances. At death these occur in gross form and are much easier to recognize. Initially, your consciousness becomes somewhat vivid, but then in the white stage becomes very vivid, then it passes to a red stage, and then in the black stage it is as if a big pot has been placed over your head, and you suddenly have been encased, everything becoming absolutely black. In the forward process, you pass from the white to the red to the black to the clear light; in the backward process, you pass from the clear light to the black to the red to the white.

A subtler version of these occurs when we sleep and we dream, but they are much harder to catch hold of because they are subtler, which also means quicker, but if you are able to get hold of these and cultivate them, then when you die it is very easy, because they appear more grossly.

[b]   There is a turtle in a well, and another turtle comes from a huge lake, and they meet. The one whose home is in the well says, "Who are you?," and the other turtle says, "I am from the great lake," and they start comparing their relative homes. The one who lives in the well says, "Well, maybe your home is half the size of mine," but the other one responds, "Oh no, that is not enough. It is even bigger than your whole well." The first one thinks that this is impossible, and so both of them go off to the great lake to look at it, and when the one from the well gets to the ocean and looks at it, he is amazed, because the two are as different as sky and earth—he is so amazed that he falls over and

that the Knowledge-Bearers, Ga-rap-dor-je[150] and so forth, taught the preceptual instructions of the Great Completeness without having thought about or having realized merely this! Switching the powerful sovereign of wish-granting jewels, the thought of the Conqueror Knowledge-Bearers,[151] for the trinkets of conceptual fabrications by logicians should be known as a manifest, true sign of a bad era.[a]

The clear light self-arisen pristine wisdom is the space-like noumenon. Because it is the noumenon, which does not exist as other than emptiness and the sphere of reality, it is without causes and conditions—uncompounded. A subtle mind, however, is a compounded phenomenon, and thus there are limitless fallacies:

- It must be produced from the four conditions; hence, it must be examined what its four conditions are, and in particular what its observed-object-condition is.
- If such [a subtle mind] is not continuous from begin-ningless time through the end, it would not be a fun-damental mind.
- If it is continuous from beginningless time through the end, then if a compounded mind not polluted by coarse conceptuality exists in the continuums of all sentient beings, does it know, or does it not know, the objects of coarse minds? If it does, why are desire and so forth not generated in it? If it does not know the

---

dies. In the same way, those who identify this mutable subtle consciousness as the Great Completeness are trying to compare it to the inconceivable huge Great Completeness.

[a]   Calling a subtle mind the Great Completeness is like switch-ing this best of wish-granting jewels for the fake jewelry that is the conceptual fabrications of those who are addicted to superfi-cial reasoning, or to words. Such switching should be known as a manifestation showing that this is a bad era.

objects of coarse minds, how could it train newly in the coarse objects of understanding involved in analyzing emptiness and thereupon meditate on emptiness?

• When a Foe Destroyer has entered into cessation, has this subtle consciousness ceased or not? If it has ceased, it is not fundamental, since it is affected by conditions. If it has not ceased, a continuum of this fundamental compounded mind would exist at the time of the nirvāṇa in which there is no remainder of mental and physical aggregates.

• Similarly, at Buddhahood this continuum of moments would not be reversed, whereby the causes of aggregates that have a mental nature would not have disappeared.

and so forth.

Moreover, in terms of the mode of appearance, as was mentioned earlier, from the level of a common being through to the Buddha ground, abandonments and realizations improve and improve; therefore, [that progress] also is not suitable to be other than from the gradual cultivation of the path within the streams of the consciousnesses of the eight collections in the continuum of the meditator.[a] Hence, mainly that must be done by the mental consciousness, and therefore, since mental awarenesses, being produced from three conditions (object, sense power, and a consciousness) have production and cessation,[b] then

---

[a] Effort and exertion must be made in order to bring about progress in the path, and this has to be done in the mind. There is not any other suitable way that it could be done.

[b] This is the case with all of our sense consciousnesses—there is an object, a sense power, and a previous moment of consciousness that act as the causes of a sense consciousness. Through the coming together of these we develop attachment and so on, and are drawn to cyclic existence—bad transmigrations, and so forth.

sometimes one meditates, and sometimes one does not meditate, and when one does meditate, it lasts for a certain period, and does not exist outside of that period, and so forth. There is no other way for it to occur, due to which it is not suitable except to assert that the path is compounded.[a]

Consequently, since the basal Great Completeness is the mode of subsistence, basic knowledge, and is uncompounded, all awarenesses and all phenomena do not pass beyond being within the state of that uncompounded mode of subsistence. However, if, in consideration of this, you assert that the path is uncompounded, then it is not necessary to mention that there would be limitless fallacies such as that you would have to assert that the person who is the meditator and all awarenesses that are the means of meditation would be uncompounded.

Objection:[b] If this which is called "path" is naked basic knowledge and emptiness at the time of meditative equipoise abiding within the state of that basic knowledge or, in accordance with the path of method,[c] is the natural clear light basic knowledge at the time of practicing the clear light appearing at the end of the three appearances,[d] how could this—in which there is not even a speck of something to be apprehended as object and subject—be designated as compounded?

---

[a]   You are practicing this path now, that path later; you are giving up this one, moving on to that one, and so forth, and therefore the paths are compounded.

[b]   This person is confusing the view with the path, and speaking of factors associated with the view as if they were the path.

[c]   That is to say, the path of the father tantras, such as the *Guhyasamāja.*

[d]   At the end of the white, red, and black appearances the mind of clear light manifests.

Answer: If this is considered from the viewpoint of the noumenon, it is not observed as either a compounded thing or an uncompounded non-thing. The noumenon, not abiding in the polarity of the compounded and the uncompounded, is to be known by oneself individually and is indeed immutable, not undergoing change even in any of the three times. However, since this is a person whose predispositions for dualistic appearance of apprehended-object and apprehending-subject with respect to the eight collections of consciousness have not been extinguished or, in the religious vocabulary of the path of method, since this is a person whose predispositions for the unfolding of the three appearances have not been extinguished, this, therefore, is an occasion of the path in which the primordial noumenon has not been released from adventitious defilements. At such a point all states of meditative equipoise and states subsequent to meditative equipoise in the continuum of the meditator do not pass beyond appearing in a continuum of moments. Hence, in terms of the mode of appearance [in such a situation, the "path"] is expressed as being compounded.

When the predispositions for the unfolding of the three appearances have been extinguished, this being at the time of Buddhahood, when the primordial noumenon manifests, the body of pristine wisdom—a great permanence like a vajra never fluctuating from the sphere of reality—is a great uncompoundedness; it is not compounded.

You will be freed from the nets of doubt when you make distinctions concerning individual intended meanings in accordance with the general scriptures such as when:

- in terms of its mode of appearance, it is posited as like being newly arisen from the viewpoint of being a

separative effect of earlier having meditatively culti-
vated the path;
- and by way of the factor of engaging in sequence in
the exalted activities of a Buddha for the sake of trainees, it is posited as like compounded, and so forth.

In that fashion, most of the others [that is, most of those
outside Ñying-ma] also assert that a Buddha body and
pristine wisdom are impermanent in entity but permanent
in terms of their continuum [in the sense that their continuums go on forever. However,] those who assert that [a
Buddha] body and pristine wisdom are a nature of frui-
tional emptiness endowed with all supreme aspects assert
that [a Buddha's] body and pristine wisdom are permanent
by way of their own entities, but impermanent and continuous in terms of how they appear to trainees, like what
is said in the *Compendium of the Thought of the Sūtras.*[a]

Thus, while—in terms of how the mode of subsistence
is—there are not any phenomena included within the
three times that deviate from the sameness of lacking production and cessation in their basic disposition, there is an
unconfused dawning of all varieties of phenomena, such as
self and other, cyclic existence and nirvāṇa, compounded
and uncompounded, past, present, and future, and so
forth. It is not necessary from apprehending one of these
two classes to abandon the other.[b] Those for whom the
import of the non-contradiction of the two truths dawns
thus in connection with the mode of realization of the

---

[a] The continuum of the reality of Buddhahood is permanent,
but in terms of how this manifests to trainees, it seems to be impermanent.

[b] Apprehending the noumenon, it is not necessary to give up
compounded phenomena, and apprehending compounded phenomena, it is not necessary to give up the noumenon.

eight profundities[a] come to have no doubt regarding the
sūtras and tantras of the Great Vehicle.[b]

> Alas, at this present time of degeneration of the
>   view,[c]
> Most of the beings who could serve as witnesses
>   have flowed into the sphere of peace.
> Those of bad conceptualization, lacking analysis
>   differentiating between what is and is not the
>   doctrine,
> Have disturbed this supreme teaching.
>
> Hungry ghosts see even food endowed with a
>   hundred tastes as awful vomit,
> And in the perspective of those with a bile disease
>   a conch appears to be yellow;
> Just so, how awful is this situation in which
> The doctrine is infected with the faults of their
>   own minds!

---

[a]   These are the eight eliminations of proliferation—the lack of
cessation, production, annihilation, permanence, coming, going,
difference, and sameness.

[b]   For beginners, the two truths appear to be contradictory,
but those persons to whom the meaning of the non-
contradiction of the two truths dawns well in this way easily generate ascertaining knowledge without doubt with respect to the
import of the sūtras and tantras.

   That concludes the text of the first book of the three cycles
concerning fundamental mind, called *The Meaning of Fundamental Mind, Clear Light, Expressed in Accordance with the
Transmission of Conqueror Knowledge-Bearers: Vajra Matrix*.

[c]   With "alas" he expresses sadness because people are not
practicing the view, meditation, and behavior of this system.

Look at this shameless assertion
That a momentary, impermanent, mutable, subtle
 mind
Which is an illustration of a true suffering
Is the path and effect of the monarch of supreme
 secrecy.

Though the Conquerors have caused the cool rain
 of the supreme doctrine—
Profound, peaceful, devoid of proliferation, luminous, uncompounded,
And like ambrosia—to fall on the realms of trainees,
It has been wrecked by the salty filth of those of
 bad lot.

Since all dualistic and conceptual proliferations
 are essentially pure, the extreme of existence is
 cleared away,
And through spontaneous self-luminosity the extreme of annihilation is cleared away.
Though expressed dualistically, it is non-dual
 equality,
Union, basic knowledge and emptiness, fundamental vajra-mind.

This is the essence of the profound thought of the
 sūtras and tantras of definitive meaning,
Unraveled well by millions of scholar-adept
 Knowledge-Bearers.
The groups of Conquerors and superior Con-
 queror-Children enlightened
From this supreme path as their basis of release are
 the witnesses.

Through the fervent intention of my own mind, I[a]
    have collected in one place
The essence of the sacred word of the omniscient
    Mi-pam,
Sole lion of proponents in the snowy ranges, ap-
    pearance of Mañjughosha,
Sole father of all Conquerors, in the manner of a
    virtuous spiritual guide for transmigrators such
    as myself.

In this that I have assembled
There is no pollution by the mess of my own
    words,
But because my qualities of training and medita-
    tive familiarization are slight,
If there are any mistakes, such as confusing the
    earlier and the later, and so forth, I confess.

Through the stainless intense virtue arisen from
    this,
Very white like a moon of autumn,
May all the pangs of fever of decline in this age of
    the five ruinations be pacified,
And may the grove of night lilies of the Subduer's
    teaching blossom.

Through the lion's roar of the supreme doctrine of
    this greatly luminous definite secrecy,
May this good text bring the auspiciousness of joy
    to the worlds of the three levels[b]

---

[a]   The person who wrote down this text was She-chen Gye-
dzal (*zhe chen dgyes rtsal*), not Mi-pam-gya-tso himself.

[b]   Below, on, and above the ground, or desire, form, and formless realms.

For as long as this great earth lasts,
Like a sun and moon lamp in darkness.

In this first book on fundamental mind, which was bestowed by the foremost lama, the omniscient, greatly perceiving Mi-pam-jam- bel-gyay-bay-dor-je,[152] I have filled in
a little from scattered notes on that foremost one's teachings. In accordance with whatever I could figure out with
my own mind I, a mantrika monastic, the stupid Dor-je-
wang-chok-gye-ba-dzel,[a] wrote this in my own place of
residence, Place of the Spreading and Propagation of the
Two Teachings,[153] during interstices between retreat ses-
sions in an isolation hut. May this also serve as a cause for
the long stability of the victory banner of the teaching of
the definitively secret.

[Publisher's Colophon]

Through the virtue of publishing this distilled es-
    sence of the secret speech of the omniscient
    lama,
May all sentient beings, transmigrators equal to
    space, myself and others,
Be taken care of by the supreme lama[b] and there-
    upon
Become monarchs of doctrine spontaneously
    achieving the two aims.[c]

---

[a] *rdo rje dbang mchog dgyes pa rtsal,* which is the poetic name
of She-chen Gye-dzal.

[b] That is to say, Mi-pam-gya-tso.

[c] "Two aims" (*don gnyis*) could be taken as the body of attributes which is the fulfillment of one's own welfare and the form
bodies which are the fulfillment of others' welfare.

Glossary

English	Tibetan	Sanskrit
abbot	mkhan po	
actual	rang mtshan pa	
apprehended-objects and apprehending-subjects	gzung 'dzin	
artifice	rtsal	
basic knowledge	rig pa	
clear light	'od gsal	
compounded	'dus byas	saṃskṛta
Conqueror Knowledge-Bearer	rgyal ba rig 'dzin	
delicate clear light	srab mo'i 'od gsal	
element of attributes/ sphere of reality	chos kyi dbyings	dharmadhātu
emptiness	stong pa nyid	śūnyatā
empty and luminous	stong gsal	
essential purity	ka dag	
fundamental cognition	gnyug ma'i yid	
fundamental mind	gnyug ma'i sems/ gnyug sems	
Great Completeness	rdzogs chen	
great seal	phyag rgya chen po	mahāmudrā
immutable mind	mi 'gyur ba'i sems	
Knowledge-Bearer	rig 'dzin	
leap-over	thod rgal	
luminous and knowing	gsal rig	
mark	mtshan ma	
master	slob dpon	
mind-basis-of-all	kun gzhi rnam par shes pa	ālayavijñāna
mind-vajra	sems kyi rdo rje	
natural mind of clear light	rang bzhin 'od gsal ba'i sems	

English	Tibetan	Sanskrit
naturally flowing noumenon	rang bzhin bab kyi chos nyid	
noumenal fundamental mind	chos nyid gnyug ma'i sems	
noumenal mind	chos nyid kyi sems	
noumenon	chos nyid	dharmatā
One-Gone-Thus	de bzhin gshegs pa	tathāgata
One-Gone-to-Bliss	bde bar gshegs pa	sugata
phenomena and noumenon	chos dang chos nyid	
pristine wisdom of clear light	'od gsal ba'i ye shes	
proliferation	spros pa	prapañca
reading-transmission	bshad lung	
reasoning of dependence	ltos pa'i rigs pa	apekṣāyukti
reasoning of nature	chos nyid kyi rigs/rig pa	dharmatāyukti
reasoning of performance of function	bya ba byed pa'i rigs pa	kāryakāraṇayukti
reasoning of tenable proof	'thad pas sgrub pa'i rigs pa	upapatti-sādhanayukti
sciences	rig gnas	
self-arisen matrix	rang byung snying po	
self-arisen pristine wisdom	rang byung ye shes	
self-dawning	rang shar	
self-effulgence	rang mdangs	
self-knowing	rang rig	
self-luminous	rang gsal	
self-release	rang grol	
sphere of reality/ element of attributes	chos kyi dbyings	dharmadhātu
sphere	dbyings	
spontaneity	lhun grub	
that endowed with the space-vajra pervading space	mkha' khyab mkha' yi rdo rje can	
Translated Word of Buddha	bka' 'gyur	
uncompounded	'dus ma byas	asaṃskṛta
unhindered	zang thal	

List of Abbreviations

"Dharma" refers to the *sde dge* edition of the Tibetan canon published by Dharma Press: the *Nyingma Edition of the sDe-dge bKa'-'gyur and bsTan-'gyur* (Oakland, Calif.: Dharma Press, 1981).

"Golden Reprint" refers to the *gser bris bstan 'gyur* (Sichuan, China: krung go'i mtho rim nang bstan slob gling gi bod brgyud nang bstan zhib 'jug khang, 1989).

"Karmapa *sde dge*" refers to the *sde dge mtshal par bka' 'gyur: A Facsimile Edition of the 18th Century Redaction of Si tu chos kyi 'byung gnas Prepared under the Direction of H.H. the 16th rgyal dbang karma pa* (Delhi: Delhi Karmapae Chodhey Gyalwae Sungrab Partun Khang, 1977).

"P," standing for "Peking edition," refers to *The Tibetan Tripitaka* (Tokyo-Kyoto: Tibetan Tripitaka Research Foundation, 1955-1962).

"*stog* Palace" refers to the *Tog Palace Manuscript of the Tibetan Kanjur* (Leh, Ladakh: Smanrtsis Shesrig Dpemdzod, 1979).

"THDL" refers to The Tibetan and Himalayan Digital Library of the University of Virginia at www.thdl.org. (The identifications in the endnotes of THDL numbers for tantras are tentative.)

"Toh" refers to *A Complete Catalogue of the Tibetan Buddhist Canons,* edited by Hakuju Ui et al. (Sendai, Japan: Tohoku University, 1934), and *A Catalogue of the Tohoku University Collection of Tibetan Works on Buddhism,* edited by Yensho Kanakura et al. (Sendai, Japan: Tohoku University, 1953).

"Tokyo *sde dge*" refers to the *sDe dge Tibetan Tripitaka—bsTan ḥgyur preserved at the Faculty of Letters, University of Tokyo,* edited by Z. Yamaguchi et al. (Tokyo: Tokyo University Press, 1977-1984).

Bibliography

Sūtras and tantras are listed alphabetically by English title in the first section of the bibliography. Indian and Tibetan treatises are listed alphabetically by author in the second section; other works are listed alphabetically by author in the third section. Works mentioned in the first or second section are not repeated in the third section.

1. Sūtras and Tantras

All-Creating Monarch
> kun byed rgyal po/ chos thams cad rdzogs pa chen po byang chub kyi sems
> kun byed rgyal po
> THDL Ng1.1.2.1

Compilations of Indicative Verse
> udānavarga
> ched du brjod pa'i tshom
> P992, vol. 39
> English translation: W. Woodville Rockhill. *The Udānavarga: A Collection of Verses from the Buddhist Canon.* London: Trübner, 1883. Also: Gareth Sparham. *The Tibetan Dhammapada.* New Delhi: Mahayana Publications, 1983; rev. ed., London: Wisdom Publications, 1986.

Compendium of the Thought of the Sūtras
> mdo dgongs pa 'dus pa/ de bzhin gshegs pa thams cad kyi dgongs pa 'dus pa'i rgyud
> THDL Ng2.3.3

Descent into Laṅkā Sūtra
> laṅkāvatārasūtra
> lang kar gshegs pa'i mdo
> P775, vol. 29
> Sanskrit: Bunyiu Nanjio. *Bibl. Otaniensis,* vol. 1. Kyoto: Otani University Press, 1923. Also: P. L. Vaidya. *Saddharmalaṅkāvatārasūtram.* Buddhist Sanskrit Texts 3. Darbhanga, India: Mithila Institute, 1963.
> English translation: D. T. Suzuki. *The Lankavatara Sutra.* London: Routledge and Kegan Paul, 1932.

Foremost Powerful Excellent Great Completeness Tantra
> rdzogs pa chen po rje btsan dam pa
> THDL Ng4.1.16

General Tantra of the Great Lotus Sovereign Gone to Bliss
> padma dbang chen bde gshegs spyi dril gyi rgyud/ de bzhin gshegs pa thams
> cad kyi dgongs pa spyi dril gyi rgyud
> THDL Ng2.3.4

Great Completeness Lion of the Culmination of Artifice Tantra
> rdzogs chen seng ge rtsal rdzogs kyi rgyud/ seng ge rtsal rdzogs chen po'i
> rgyud
> THDL Ng1.3.3.8

Guhyasamāja Tantra
> sarvatathāgatakāyavākcittarahasyaguhyasamājanāmamahākalparāja
> de bzhin gshegs pa thams cad kyi sku gsung thugs kyi gsang chen gsang ba
> 'dus pa zhes bya ba brtag pa'i rgyal po chen po
> P81, vol. 3; D442, vol. ca; Dharma vol. 29

Hevajra Tantra
> hevajratantrarāja
> kye'i rdo rje zhes bya ba rgyud kyi rgyal po
> P10, vol. 1
> English translation: D. L. Snellgrove. *Hevajra Tantra*, Parts 1 and 2. Lon-
> don: Oxford University Press, 1959. Also: G. W. Farrow and I. Menon.
> *The Concealed Essence of the Hevajra Tantra*. Delhi: Motilal Banarsidass,
> 1992.

Inlaid Jewels Tantra
> nor bu phra bkod/ nor bu phra bkod rang gi don thams cad gsal bar byed
> pa'i rgyud
> THDL Ng1.3.3.16

Mad Elephant Tantra
> glang po rab 'bog gi rgyud
> THDL Ng3.1.3.3.5

Miraculous Secret Essence
> sgyu 'phrul gsang ba snying po
> THDL Ng3.1.1.8

Miraculous Transcendence Great Tantra
> sgyu 'phrul thal ba'i rgyud chen po
> THDL Ng3.1.2.1.4

Mirror of the All-Good Exalted Mind Tantra
> kun tu bzang po thugs kyi me long gi rgyud
> THDL Ng1.3.3.14

Monarch of Multitudinous Expanse Tantra
> klong chen rab 'byams rgyal po'i rgyud
> THDL Ng1.2.1

Monarch of Tantras: The Vajrasattva Magical Net
> rgyud kyi rgyal po rdo rje sems dpa' sgyu 'phrul dra ba/ rdo rje sems dpa'i
> sgyu 'phrul dra ba gsang ba thams cad kyi me long zhes bya ba'i rgyud
> THDL Ng3.1.2.1.2

Quintessence of the View of the Great Completeness: The Broad Expanse of Space Tantra
> rdzogs pa chen po lta ba'i yang snying nam mkha' klong yangs kyi rgyud
> THDL Ng1.5.20

Tantra Containing the Definitive Meaning of the Great Completeness
> rdzogs chen nges don 'dus pa'i rgyud/ lta ba thams cad kyi snying po rin po che rnam par bkod pa
> THDL Ng1.5.17

Tantra of the Expanse of the All-Good Pristine Wisdom: Refined Gold of Great Value
> kun tu bzang po ye shes klong gi rgyud rin chen gser gyi yang zhun/ rdzogs pa chen po nges don 'dus pa'i yang snying
> THDL Ng1.5.23

Tantra of Great Luminous Meaning Devoid of Proliferation
> spros bral don gsal chen po'i rgyud
> THDL Ng1.5.1

Tantra of the Great Completeness Equal to Space
> rdzogs chen nam mkha' dang mnyam pa'i rgyud
> THDL Ng1.5.24

Tantra of Quintessential Instructions of the Precious Lamp of Secret Pristine Wisdom
> ye shes gsang ba'i sgron ma rin po che man ngag gi rgyud
> THDL Ng1.2.7

Tantra of the Great Self-Dawning Basic Knowledge
> rig pa rang shar chen po'i rgyud
> THDL Ng1.3.3.3

Tantra of the View of the Great Completeness: The Complete Depth of Pristine Wisdom
> rdzogs chen lta ba ye shes gting rdzogs kyi rgyud
> THDL Ng1.1.3.21

2. Other Sanskrit and Tibetan Works

Anubhūtisvarūpācārya
> *Sarasvatī's Grammar Sūtra*
> sārasvatavyākaraṇa / sārasvatīprakriyā
> dbyangs can sgra mdo/ dbyangs can ma
> P5886, vol. 148; P5911, vol. 149; P5912, vol. 149

Āryadeva (*'phags pa lha*, second to third century C.E.)
> *Four Hundred / Treatise of Four Hundred Stanzas / Four Hundred Stanzas on the Yogic Deeds of Bodhisattvas*
> catuḥśatakaśāstrakārikā
> bstan bcos bzhi brgya pa zhes bya ba'i tshig le'ur byas pa
> P5246, vol. 95
> Edited Tibetan and Sanskrit fragments along with English translation:

Karen Lang. *Āryadeva's Catuḥśataka: On the Bodhisattva's Cultivation of Merit and Knowledge.* Indiske Studier 7. Copenhagen: Akademisk Forlag, 1986.

English translation: Geshe Sonam Rinchen and Ruth Sonam. *Yogic Deeds of Bodhisattvas: Gyel-tsap on Āryadeva's Four Hundred.* Ithaca, N.Y.: Snow Lion Publications, 1994.

Italian translation of the last half from the Chinese: Giuseppe Tucci. "Studi Mahāyānici: La versione cinese del Catuḥśataka di Āryadeva, confronta col testo sanscrito e la traduzione tibetana." *Rivista degli Studi Orientali* 10 (1925): 521-567.

Asaṅga (*thogs med,* fourth century)

Five Treatises on the Grounds

1. *Grounds of Yogic Practice*
   yogācārabhūmi
   rnal 'byor spyod pa'i sa
   P5536-5538, vols. 109-110

   Grounds of Bodhisattvas
   bodhisattvabhūmi
   byang chub sems pa'i sa
   P5538, vol. 110

   Sanskrit: Unrai Wogihara. *Bodhisattvabhūmi: A Statement of the Whole Course of the Bodhisattva (Being the Fifteenth Section of Yogācārabhūmi).* Leipzig: 1908; Tokyo: Seigo Kenyūkai, 1930-1936. Also: Nalinaksha Dutt. *Bodhisattvabhumi (Being the XVth Section of Asangapada's Yogacarabhumi).* Tibetan Sanskrit Works Series 7. Patna, India: K. P. Jayaswal Research Institute, 1966.

   English translation of the Chapter on Suchness, the fourth chapter of Part I of what is the fifteenth volume of the *Grounds of Yogic Practice:* Janice D. Willis. *On Knowing Reality.* New York: Columbia University Press, 1979; reprint, Delhi: Motilal Banarsidass, 1979.

2. *Compendium of Ascertainments*
   nirṇayasaṃgraha / viniścayasaṃgrahaṇī
   rnam par gtan la dbab pa bsdu ba
   P5539, vols. 110-111

3. *Compendium of Bases*
   vastusaṃgraha
   gzhi bsdu ba
   P5540, vol. 111

4. *Compendium of Enumerations*
   paryāyasaṃgraha
   rnam grang bsdu ba
   P5543, vol. 111

5. *Compendium of Explanations*
   vivaraṇasaṃgraha
   rnam par bshad pa bsdu ba

P5543, vol. 111

Grounds of Hearers
nyan sa
śrāvakabhūmi
P5537, vol. 110
Sanskrit: Karunesha Shukla. *Śrāvakabhūmi.* Tibetan Sanskrit Works Series 14. Patna, India: K. P. Jayaswal Research Institute, 1973.

Two Summaries

1. *Summary of Manifest Knowledge*
abhidharmasamuccaya
chos mngon pa kun btus
P5550, vol. 112
Sanskrit: Pralhad Pradhan. *Abhidharma Samuccaya of Asaṅga.* Visva-Bharati Series 12. Santiniketan, India: Visva-Bharati (Santiniketan Press), 1950.
French translation: Walpola Rahula. *La compendium de la super-doctrine (philosophie) (Abhidharmasamuccaya) d'Asaṅga.* Paris: École Française d'Extrême-Orient, 1971.
English translation: Walpola Rahula. *Abhidharmasamuccaya: The Compendium of the Higher Teaching (Philosophy) by Asaṅga.* Trans. Sara Boin-Webb. Fremont, Calif.: Asian Humanities Press, 2001.

2. *Summary of the Great Vehicle*
mahāyānasaṃgraha
theg pa chen po bsdus pa
P5549, vol. 112
French translation and Chinese and Tibetan texts: Étienne Lamotte. *La somme du grand véhicule d'Asaṅga.* 2 vols. Publications de l'Institute Orientaliste de Louvain 8. Louvain: Université de Louvain, 1938; reprint, 1973.
English translation: John P. Keenan. *The Summary of the Great Vehicle by Bodhisattva Asaṅga: Translated from the Chinese of Paramārtha.* Berkeley, Calif.: Numata Center for Buddhist Translation and Research, 1992.

Ba-ri Lo-sang-rap-šel (*dpa' ris blo bzang rab gsal,* 1840-1910?)
Rap-sel's Response to Refutations
rab gsal dgag lan
n.d.

Chandragomin
Chandragomin's Grammar
lung du ston pa cāndra pa'i mdo
P5767, vol. 140
Sanskrit edition: *Cāndravyākaraṇam.* Jodhapura, 1967.

Chandrakīrti (*candrakīrti, zla ba grags pa,* seventh century)
[Auto]commentary on the "Supplement to (Nāgārjuna's) 'Treatise on the Middle'"
madhaymakāvatārabhāṣya
dbu ma la 'jug pa'i bshad pa / dbu ma la 'jug pa'i rang 'grel

P5263, vol. 98. Also: Dharmsala, India: Council of Religious and Cultural Affairs, 1968.

Tibetan: Louis de La Vallée Poussin. *Madhyamakāvatāra par Candrakīrti*. Bibliotheca Buddhica 9. Osnabrück, Germany: Biblio Verlag, 1970.

English translation: C. W. Huntington, Jr. *The Emptiness of Emptiness: An Introduction to Early Indian Mādhyamika*, 147-195. Honolulu: University of Hawaii Press, 1989.

French translation (up to chap. 6, stanza 165): Louis de La Vallée Poussin. *Muséon* 8 (1907): 249-317; *Muséon* 11 (1910): 271-358; *Muséon* 12 (1911): 235-328.

German translation (chap. 6, stanzas 166-226): Helmut Tauscher. *Candrakīrti-Madhyamakāvatāraḥ und Madhyamakāvatārabhāṣyam*. Vienna: Arbeitskreis für Tibetische und Buddhistische Studien, Universität Wien, 1981.

Supplement to (Nāgārjuna's) "Treatise on the Middle"
madhyamakāvatāra
dbu ma la 'jug pa
P5261, P5262, vol. 98

Tibetan: Louis de La Vallée Poussin. *Madhyamakāvatāra par Candrakīrti*. Bibliotheca Buddhica 9. Osnabrück, Germany: Biblio Verlag, 1970.

English translation (chaps. 1-5): Jeffrey Hopkins. *Compassion in Tibetan Buddhism*. London: Rider, 1980; reprint, Ithaca, N.Y.: Snow Lion Publications, 1980.

English translation (chap. 6): Stephen Batchelor. *Echoes of Voidness* by Geshé Rabten, 47-92. London: Wisdom Publications, 1983.

See also references under Chandrakīrti's *[Auto]commentary on the "Supplement."*

Dharmakīrti (*chos kyi grags pa*, seventh century)

Seven Treatises on Valid Cognition

1. *Analysis of Relations*
   sambandhaparīkṣā
   'brel pa brtag pa
   P5713, vol. 130

2. *Ascertainment of Prime Cognition*
   pramāṇaviniścaya
   tshad ma rnam par nges pa
   P5710, vol. 130

3. *Commentary on (Dignāga's) "Compilation of Prime Cognition"*
   pramāṇavārttikakārikā
   tshad ma rnam 'grel gyi tshig le'ur byas pa
   P5709, vol. 130. Also: Sarnath, India: Pleasure of Elegant Sayings Press, 1974.
   Sanskrit: Dwarikadas Shastri. *Pramāṇavārttika of Āchārya Dharmakīrtti*. Varanasi, India: Bauddha Bharati, 1968. Also, Yūsho Miyasaka. "Pramāṇavarttika-Kārikā (Sanskrit and Tibetan)," *Acta Indologica* 2 (1971-1972): 1-206. Also, (chap. 1 and autocommentary) Raniero

Gnoli. *The Pramāṇavārttikam of Dharmakīrti: The First Chapter with the Autocommentary.* Rome: Istituto Italiano per il Medio ed Estremo Oriente, 1960.

English translation (chap. 2): Masatoshi Nagatomi. "A Study of Dharmakīrti's Pramāṇavarttika: An English Translation and Annotation of the Pramāṇavarttika, Book I." Ph.D. diss., Harvard University, 1957.

English translation (chap. 4, stanzas 1-148): Tom J.F. Tillemans. *Dharmakīrti's Pramāṇavārttika: An Annotated Translation of the Fourth Chapter (parārthānumāna),* vol. 1. Vienna: Verlag der Österreichischen Akademie der Wissenschaften, 2000.

4. *Drop of Reasoning*
   nyāyabinduprakaraṇa
   rigs pa'i thigs pa zhes bya ba'i rab tu byed pa
   P5711, vol. 130

   English translation: Th. Stcherbatsky. *Buddhist Logic.* New York: Dover Publications, 1962.

5. *Drop of Reasons*
   hetubindunāmaprakaraṇa
   gtan tshigs kyi thigs pa zhes bya ba rab tu byed pa
   P5712, vol. 130

6. *Principles of Debate*
   vādanyāya
   rtsod pa'i rigs pa
   P5715, vol. 130

7. *Proof of Other Continuums*
   saṃtānāntarasiddhināmaprakaraṇa
   rgyud gzhan grub pa zhes bya ba'i rab tu byed pa
   P5716, vol. 130

Guṇaprabha (*yon tan 'od*)
   Aphorisms on Discipline
   vinayasūtra
   'dul ba'i mdo
   P5619, vol. 123

Maitreya (*byams pa*)
Five Doctrines of Maitreya
1. *Sublime Continuum of the Great Vehicle / Great Vehicle Treatise on the Sublime Continuum / Treatise on the Later Scriptures of the Great Vehicle*
   mahāyānottaratantraśāstra
   theg pa chen po rgyud bla ma'i bstan bcos
   P5525, vol. 108; D4024, Dharma vol. 77

   Sanskrit: E. H. Johnston (and T. Chowdhury). *The Ratnagotravibhāga Mahāyānottaratantraśāstra.* Patna, India: Bihar Research Society, 1950.

   English translation: E. Obermiller. "Sublime Science of the Great Vehicle to Salvation." *Acta Orientalia* 9 (1931): 81-306. Also: J. Takasaki. *A Study on the Ratnagotravibhāga.* Rome: Istituto Italiano per il Medio ed Estremo Oriente, 1966.

2. *Differentiation of Phenomena and Noumenon*
dharmadharmatāvibhaṅga
chos dang chos nyid rnam par 'byed pa
P5523, vol. 108; D4022, Dharma vol. 77

Edited Tibetan: Jōshō Nozawa. "The *Dharmadharmatāvibhaṅga* and the *Dharmadharmatā-vibhaṅgavṛtti*, Tibetan Texts, Edited and Collated, Based upon the Peking and Derge Editions." In *Studies in Indology and Buddhology: Presented in Honour of Professor Susumu Yamaguchi on the Occasion of his Sixtieth Birthday*, edited by Gadjin M. Nagao and Jōshō Nozawa. Kyoto: Hozokan, 1955.

English translation: John Younghan Cha. "A Study of the *Dharmadharmatāvibhāga*: An Analysis of the Religious Philosophy of the Yogācāra, Together with an Annotated Translation of Vasubandhu's Commentary." Ph.D. diss., Northwestern University, 1996.

English translation: Jim Scott. *Maitreya's Distinguishing Phenomena and Pure Being with commentary by Mipham*. Ithaca, N.Y.: Snow Lion Publications, 2004.

3. *Differentiation of the Middle and the Extremes*
madhyāntavibhaṅga
dbus dang mtha' rnam par 'byed pa
P5522, vol. 108; D4021, Dharma vol. 77

Sanskrit: Gadjin M. Nagao. *Madhyāntavibhāga-bhāsya*. Tokyo: Suzuki Research Foundation, 1964. Also: Ramchandra Pandeya. *Madhyāntavibhāga-śāstra*. Delhi: Motilal Banarsidass, 1971.

English translation: Stefan Anacker. *Seven Works of Vasubandhu*. Delhi: Motilal Banarsidass, 1984.

Also, of chapter 1: Thomas A. Kochumuttom. *A Buddhist Doctrine of Experience*. Delhi: Motilal Banarsidass, 1982. Also, of chapter 1: Th. Stcherbatsky. *Madhyāntavibhāga, Discourse on Discrimination between Middle and Extremes Ascribed to Bodhisattva Maitreya and Commented by Vasubandhu and Sthiramati*. Bibliotheca Buddhica 30 (1936). Osnabrück, Germany: Biblio Verlag, 1970; reprint, Calcutta: Indian Studies Past and Present, 1971. Also, of chapter 1: David Lasar Friedmann. *Sthiramati, Madhyāntavibhāgaṭīkā: Analysis of the Middle Path and the Extremes*. Utrecht, Netherlands: Rijksuniversiteit te Leiden, 1937. Also, of chapter 3: Paul Wilfred O'Brien, S.J. "A Chapter on Reality from the Madhyāntavibhāgaśāstra." *Monumenta Nipponica* 9, nos. 1-2 (1953): 277-303 and *Monumenta Nipponica* 10, nos. 1-2 (1954): 227-269.

4. *Ornament for Clear Realization*
abhisamayālaṃkāra
mngon par rtogs pa'i rgyan
P5184, vol. 88; D3786, vol. ka; Dharma vol. 63

Sanskrit: Th. Stcherbatsky and E. Obermiller, eds. *Abhisamayālaṃkāra-Prajñāpāramitā-Upadeśa-Śāstra*. Bibliotheca Buddhica 23. Osnabrück, Germany: Biblio Verlag, 1970.

English translation: Edward Conze. *Abhisamayālaṃkāra*. Serie Orientale
  Roma 6. Rome: Istituto Italiano per il Medio ed Estremo Oriente,
  1954.

5. *Ornament for the Great Vehicle Sūtras*
  mahāyānasūtrālaṃkāra
  theg pa chen po'i mdo sde rgyan gyi tshig le'ur byas pa
  P5521, vol. 108; D4020, Dharma vol. 77

  Sanskrit: Sitansusekhar Bagchi. *Mahāyāna-Sūtrālaṃkāraḥ of Asaṅga* [with
    Vasubandhu's commentary]. Buddhist Sanskrit Texts 13. Darbhanga,
    India: Mithila Institute, 1970.

  Sanskrit text and translation into French: Sylvain Lévi. *Mahāyāna-
    Sūtrālaṃkāra, exposé de la doctrine du Grand Véhicule selon le système
    Yogācāra*. 2 vols. Paris: Bibliothèque de l'École des Hautes Études,
    1907, 1911.

  English translation: L. Jamspal et al. *The Universal Vehicle Discourse Litera-
    ture*. Editor-in-chief, Robert A.F Thurman. New York: American Insti-
    tute of Buddhist Studies, Columbia University, 2004.

Mi-pam-gya-tso (*mi pham rgya mtsho*, 1846-1912)
  *Clear Exposition of the Text of (Dharmakīrti's) "Commentary on (Dignāga's)
    'Compilation of Prime Cognition'": Treasure Illuminating Eloquence*
  tshad ma rnam 'grel gyi gzhung gsal bor bshad pa legs bshad snang ba'i
    gter

    *Collected Writings of 'Jam-mgon 'Ju Mi-pham-rgya-mtsho : Comprising a col-
      lection of the works of the scholar-saint selected for their rarity from recently
      unpublished xylographic prints and MSS. from the libraries of Dudjom
      Rimpoche, Luding Khen Rimpoche, and other religious teachers and laymen
      by Sonam Topgay Kazi.* Gangtok: Kazi, 1972

  Explanation of the Eight Pronouncements
  bka' brgyad rnam bshad
  khreng tu'u: si khron mi rigs dpe skrun khang, 2000

    *Collected Writings of 'Jam-mgon 'Ju Mi-pham-rgya-mtsho : Comprising a col-
      lection of the works of the scholar-saint selected for their rarity from recently
      unpublished xylographic prints and MSS. from the libraries of Dudjom
      Rimpoche, Luding Khen Rimpoche, and other religious teachers and laymen
      by Sonam Topgay Kazi.* Gangtok: Kazi, 1972.

  *The Meaning of Fundamental Mind, Clear Light, Expressed in Accordance with
    the Transmission of Conqueror Knowledge-Bearers: Vajra Matrix*
  gnyug sems 'od gsal gyi don rgyal ba rig 'dzin brgyud pa'i lung bzhin brjod
    pa rdo rje'i snying po
  Edition cited: Varanasi: Tarthang Tulku, 1965.

    *Gñug sems skor gsum; and, Gzhung spyi'i dka gnad: a cycle of profound teach-
      ings upon the nature of mind and an elucidation of the most difficult points
      of Buddhist philosophy taught by 'Jam-mgon Bla-ma Mi-pham and written
      by Ze-chen Rgyal-tshab 'Gyur-med-pad-ma-rnam-rgyal.* Paro, Bhutan :
      Kyichu Temple, 1982.

    Gñug sems skor gsum: notes on 'Jam-Mgon Mi-Pham-Rgya-Mtsho's Lectures

*on the Nature of the Primordial Mind in the Context of Dzogchen
Psychology, as Transcribed by his Disciple Ze-chen Rgyal-tshab Padma-
Rnam-Rgyal.* Gangtok: Sonam Topgay Kazi, 1972.

*Collected writings of 'Jam-mgon 'Ju Mi-pham-rgya-mtsho : Comprising a col-
lection of the works of the scholar-saint selected for their rarity from recently
unpublished xylographic prints and MSS. from the libraries of Dudjom
Rimpoche, Luding Khen Rimpoche, and other religious teachers and laymen
by Sonam Topgay Kazi.* Gangtok: Kazi, 1972.

*Response to Objections Concerning the Chapter on Wisdom in (Shāntideva's)
"Engaging in the Bodhisattva Deeds": Sunshine Illumination*
spyod 'jug sher le brgal lan nyin byed snang ba

*Collected Writings of 'Jam-mgon 'Ju Mi-pham-rgya-mtsho : Comprising a col-
lection of the works of the scholar-saint selected for their rarity from recently
unpublished xylographic prints and MSS. from the libraries of Dudjom
Rimpoche, Luding Khen Rimpoche, and other religious teachers and laymen
by Sonam Topgay Kazi.* Gangtok: Kazi, 1972.

Ñga-ri Paṇ-chen Padma-wang-gyel (*mnga' ris paṇ chen padma dbang rgyal*)
Ascertainment of the Three Vows
sdom gsum rnam nges
n.d.

Ša-gya Paṇḍita (*sa skya paṇḍita kun dga' rgyal mtshan*, 1182-1251)
Treasury of Reasoning on Valid Cognition
tshad ma rigs pa'i gter

*The Complete Works of the Great Masters of the Sa-skya Sect of the Tibetan
Buddhism,* vol. 5, 155.1.1-167.2.1. Tokyo: Toyo Bunko, 1968.

Sarvarvarman
Kalāpasūtra
kalāpasūtra
ka lā pa'i mdo
P5775, vol. 140

Shāntideva (*zhi ba lha,* eighth century)
Engaging in the Bodhisattva Deeds
bodhi[sattva]caryāvatāra
byang chub sems dpa'i spyod pa la 'jug pa
P5272, vol. 99

Sanskrit: P. L. Vaidya. *Bodhicaryāvatāra.* Buddhist Sanskrit Texts 12.
Darbhanga, India: Mithila Institute, 1988.

Sanskrit and Tibetan: Vidhushekara Bhattacharya. *Bodhicaryāvatāra.* Bibliotheca Indica 280. Calcutta: Asiatic Society, 1960.

Sanskrit and Tibetan with Hindi translation: Rāmaśaṁkara Tripāṭhī, ed.
Bodhicaryāvatāra. Bauddha-Himālaya-Granthamālā, 8. Leh, Ladākh:
Central Institute of Buddhist Studies, 1989.

English translation: Stephen Batchelor. *A Guide to the Bodhisattva's Way of
Life.* Dharamsala, India: Library of Tibetan Works and Archives, 1979.
Also: Marion Matics. *Entering the Path of Enlightenment.* New York:
Macmillan, 1970. Also: Kate Crosby and Andrew Skilton. *The*

Bodhicaryāvatāra. Oxford: Oxford University Press, 1996. Also: Padmakara Translation Group. *The Way of the Bodhisattva.* Boston: Shambhala, 1997. Also: Vesna A. Wallace and B. Alan Wallace. *A Guide to the Bodhisattva Way of Life.* Ithaca, N.Y.: Snow Lion Publications, 1997.

Contemporary commentary by H.H. the Dalai Lama, Tenzin Gyatso. *Transcendent Wisdom.* Ithaca, N.Y.: Snow Lion Publications, 1988. Also: H.H. the Dalai Lama, Tenzin Gyatso. *A Flash of Lightning in the Dark of the Night.* Boston: Shambhala, 1994.

Virūpa
  Utterly Without Proliferation
  suniṣprapañcatattvopadeśa-nāma
  shin tu spros med/ shin tu spros pa med pa de kho na nyid kyi man ngag ces bya ba
  P2876, vol. 67

3. Other Works

Dorje, Gyurme, and Matthew Kapstein. *The Nyingma School of Tibetan Buddhism: Its Fundamentals and History.* Vol. 2. Boston: Wisdom Publications, 1991.

Dudjom Rinpoche. *The Nyingma School of Tibetan Buddhism: Its Fundamentals and History.* Vol. 1. Trans. and ed. Gyurme Dorje and Matthew Kapstein. Boston: Wisdom Publications, 1991.

Goodman, Steven D. "Mi-pham rgya-mtsho: An Account of His Life, the Printing of His Works, and the Structure of His Treatise Entitled *mKhas-pa'i tshul la 'jug-pa'i sgo.*" In Ronald M. Davidson (ed.), *Wind Horse: Proceedings of the North American Tibetological Society,* 58-78. Berkeley: Asian Humanities Press, 1981.

Kapstein, Matthew. "Mi-pham's Theory of Interpretation." In Donald S. Lopez, Jr. (ed.), *Buddhist Hermeneutics,* pp. 149-174. Honolulu: University of Hawaii Press, 1988.

Pettit, John. *Mi-pham's Beacon of Certainty.* Boston: Wisdom Publications, 1999.

Endnotes

[1] *gnyug sems 'od gsal gyi don rgyal ba rig 'dzin brgyud pa'i lung bzhin brjod pa rdo rje'i snying po*. I have added the chapter headings.

[2] *mi pham 'jam dbyangs rnam rgyal rgya mtsho*. His names, as listed in TBRC (Tibetan Buddhist Resource Center) P252, are *mi pham rnam rgyal rgya mtsho, mi pham rgya mtsho, 'ju mi pham rnam rgyal rgya mtsho*, and *'jam mgon mi pham rgya mtsho*.

[3] Edited and translated by Jeffrey Hopkins, co-edited by Anne C. Klein (London: Rider/Hutchinson, 1982; Ithaca, N.Y.: Snow Lion Publications, 1983; German edition, Munich: Diederichs Verlag, 1988; Chinese edition, Om Ah Hum, 1998).

[4] Dharamsala, India: Library of Tibetan Works and Archives, 1973.

[5] Dharamsala, India: Library of Tibetan Works and Archives, 1973.

[6] See "A Standard System of Tibetan Transcription," *Harvard Journal of Asian Studies*, 22 (1959): 261-267.

[7] See the technical note in Jeffrey Hopkins, *Meditation on Emptiness* (London: Wisdom Publications, 1983), pp. 19-21.

[8] This is an oral expansion, and sometimes condensation of Mi-pam-gya-tso's biography; see Khetsun Sangpo, *Biographical Dictionary of Tibet and Tibetan Buddhism,* vol. 4 (Dharamsala, India: Library of Tibetan Works and Archives, 1973), 531-547. For a splendid translation of a similar biography, as well as helpful notes, see Dudjom Rinpoche, *The Nyingma School of Tibetan Buddhism,* vol. 1, trans. and ed. Gyurme Dorje and Matthew Kapstein (Boston: Wisdom Publications, 1991), 869-880. For helpful additional material, see Steven D. Goodman, "Mi-pham rgya-mtsho: An Account of His Life, the Printing of His Works, and the Structure of His Treatise Entitled *mKhas-pa'i tshul la 'jug-pa'i sgo*," in Ronald M. Davidson (ed.), *Wind Horse: Proceedings of the North American Tibetological Society* (Berkeley: Asian Humanities Press, 1981), 58-78; and John Pettit, *Mi-pham's Beacon of Certainty* (Boston: Wisdom Publications, 1999), 19-39.

⁹   *khams.*

¹⁰   *ya chu'i ding chung;* TBRC reports that "this place is located in the present *sde dge* county, *dkar mdzes* prefecture."

¹¹   *pad ma dar rgyas.*

¹²   *mi pham rgya mtsho.*

¹³   *mnga' ris paṇ chen padma dbang rgyal.*

¹⁴   *sdom gsum rnam nges.*

¹⁵   *'ju me hor gsang sngags cho gling.*

¹⁶   *zelzhe chen bstan gnyis dar rgyas gling.*

¹⁷   *'o rgyan smin grol gling.*

¹⁸   *dbyangs 'char gyi dpe rnying.*

¹⁹   *'ju nyung.*

²⁰   *'jam dbyangs smra seng.*

²¹   *bshad lung;* these can include occasional discussion of important points but tend to be the reading of a text, constituting transmission passed down orally from another master.

²²   *rig gnas.*

²³   *nyag rong/ nyan rong.*

²⁴   *mgo log.*

²⁵   *'gyur bzang.*

²⁶   *lho brag mkhar chu.*

²⁷   *nam mkha' snying po.*

²⁸   *rje 'bangs nyer lnga;* King Tri-šong-day-dzen (*khri srong sde'u btsan*) and twenty-four "subjects."

²⁹   *kun gzigs dbyangs 'char chen mo shel gyi me long.*

³⁰   *lab skyabs mgon dbang chen dgyes rab rdo rje,* born 1832.

³¹   *makṣa'i las sbyor;* Gyurme Dorje and Matthew Kapstein (*The Nyingma School of Tibetan Buddhism,* vol. 2, 85 n. 1210) identify this as bean-sprout rites, "in which the mantra of White Mañjuśrī is recited while a dark-brown *makṣaka* bean is held in the mouth. If the bean sprouts, this is a sign of successful accomplishment."

³²   *rdza dpal sprul o rgyan 'jigs med chos kyi dbang po,* 1808-1887.

³³   *spyod 'jug shes rab le'u'i tshig don go slar bshad pa.*

³⁴   *'jam dbyangs mkhyen brtse'i dbang po,* 1820-1892.

[35] *rin chen gter mdzod.*

[36] *'jam mgon kong sprul blo gros mtha' yas/' jam mgon yon tan rgya mtsho,* 1813-1899.

[37] *cāndravyākaraṇasūtra;* P5767, vol. 140.

[38] The *Rangjung Yeshe Dictionary* lists the five as:

1. *sgra rig pa'i ming gi mtshams sbyor, śabdavidyānāmasandhi:* sandhi of grammatical terms

2. *dbyangs kyi mtshams sbyor, svara-sandhi:* sandhi of vowels

3. *rang bzhin gyi mtshams sbyor:* (?)

4. *gsal byed kyi mtshams sbyor, vyañjana-sandhi:* sandhi of consonants

5. *rnam bcad kyi mtshams sbyor, visarga-sandhi:* sandhi of visarga.

Thanks to Prof. Karen Lang for the Sanskrit and the English.

[39] *dbyangs can sgra mdo, sārasvatavyākaraṇa;* P5886, vol. 148; P5911, vol. 149; P5912, vol. 149.

[40] *ka lā pa'i mdo, kalāpasūtra;* P5775, vol. 140.

[41] *'jam dpal tshe bdag nag po/gshin rje tshe bdag nag po/'jam dpal tshe bdag lcags 'dra lcags sdig.*

[42] 1867-1934.

[43] See p. 48.

[44] The four reasonings are:

1. The reasoning of dependence (*ltos pa'i rigs pa, apekṣāyukti*) is from the viewpoint that the arising of effects depends on causes and conditions.

2. The reasoning of performance of function (*bya ba byed pa'i rigs pa, kāryakāraṇayukti*) is from the viewpoint that phenomena perform their respective functions, such as fire performing the function of burning. One examines, "This is the phenomenon; this is the functioning; it performs this function."

3. The reasoning of tenable proof (*'thad pas sgrub pa'i rigs pa, upapattisādhanayukti*) is to prove a meaning without contradicting valid cognition. It is an examination within considering whether the meaning has valid cognition—direct, inferential, or believable scripture.

4. The reasoning of nature (*chos nyid kyi rigs pa, dhar-matāyukti*) is to examine from the viewpoint of natures renowned in the world, such as heat being the nature of fire and moisture being the nature of water; inconceivable natures such as placing a world system in a single hair-pore, and so forth.

⁴⁵ *ju dbon 'jigs med rdo rje.*

⁴⁶ *'bum gsar dge bshes ngag dbang 'byung gnas.*

⁴⁷ *blo gter dbang po,* 1847-1914,

⁴⁸ *tshad ma rig gter;* in *The Complete Works of the Great Masters of the Sa-skya Sect of the Tibetan Buddhism,* vol. 5, 155.1.1-167.2.1 (Tokyo: Toyo Bunko, 1968).

⁴⁹ *sa skya paṇḍita kun dga' rgyal mtshan,* 1182-1251.

⁵⁰ *gsol dpon padma.*

⁵¹ *bka' brgyud.*

⁵² *dge lugs.*

⁵³ *dpa' ris blo bzang rab gsal,* 1840-1910(?).

⁵⁴ *rab gsal dgag lan.*

⁵⁵ *hor brag dkar sprul sku blo bzang dpal ldan bstan 'dzin snyan grags,* 1866-1928; two texts are *mi pham rnam rgyal gyi klan ka bgyis pa dang po* and *mi pham rnam rgyal gyi rtsod pa'i yang lan log lta'i khong khrag 'don pa'i skyug sman.* Thanks to Gene Smith for the identification.

⁵⁶ *spyod 'jug sher le brgal lan nyin byed snang ba.*

⁵⁷ *tshad ma rnam 'grel gyi gzhung gsal bor bshad pa legs bshad snang ba'i gter.*

⁵⁸ *'dul ba'i mdo, vinayasūtra;* P5619, vol. 123.

⁵⁹ *bka' 'gyur.* This is an enormous collection of Tibetan translations of sūtras and tantras in 108 volumes.

⁶⁰ *ngag dbang rin chen 'bar ba.*

⁶¹ *bka' brgyad rnam bshad.*

⁶² *'ja' pa mdo sngags.*

⁶³ *bla ma rig mchog.*

⁶⁴ For an extensive presentation of Mi-pam-gya-tso's opinions on this, see Chapter Three.

⁶⁵ Douglas Duckworth, on reading the manuscript for this

book, pointed to another debate in person mentioned in Karma Phuntsho, *Mipham's Dialectics and the Debates on Emptiness* (London: RoutledgeCurzon, 2005), 53:

> mKhan po 'Jigs med Phun tshogs reports a debate with Mongolian dGe lugs pa scholar Blo bzang Phun tshogs in the presence of 'Jam dbyangs mKhyen brtse'i dBang po, the rNying ma pa scholar rDo grub bsTan pa'i Nyi ma, the Sa skya scholar Blo gter dBang po, and the dGe lugs master Mi nyag Kun bzang Chos grags.

66 *klong chen rab 'byams / klong chen dri med 'od zer,* 1308-1363.

67 *thod rgal.*

68 *chos nyid.* The term refers to the final reality and is often found in the pair, phenomena and noumenon (*chos dang chos nyid*).

69 For a list of the more important students, see Dudjom Rinpoche, *Nyingma School,* vol. 1, 879, and TBRC P252.

70 *zhe chen dgyes rtsal.*

71 "Vajrasattva" is often spelled "Vajrasatva" in Tibetan texts, and thus I am using the latter in the mantras.

72 That is, father and mother, or male and female deities.

73 *'ju mi pham rgya mtsho,* 1846-1912.

74 *gnyug sems.*

75 *mi 'gyur ba'i sems.*

76 *'od gsal.*

77 *chos nyid kyi sems.*

78 *rdzogs chen.*

79 *dga' rab rdo rje.*

80 *'jam dpal gshes gnyen.*

81 *khri srong sde'u btsan.*

82 *mkhan po.*

83 *slob dpon.*

84 *rtsal.*

85 *sa skya paṇḍita kun dga' rgyal mtshan,* 1182-1251.

86 *de bzhin gshegs pa, tathāgata.*

87 *bde bar gshegs pa, sugata.*

[88]   *chos kyi dbyings.*

[89]   *spros pa, prapañca.*

[90]   *rtsod pa bzlog pa'i tshig le'ur byas pa, vigrahavyāvartanīkārikā,*
in stanza 29; P5229, vol. 95, 15.1.1. Sanskrit text in Bhattacharya, Johnston, and Kunst, *Dialectical Method,* 14 and 61: *yadi
kācana pratijñā syān me tata eṣa me bhaved doṣaḥ / nāsti ca mama
pratijñā tasmān naivāsti me doṣaḥ //.*

[91]   *mdo dgongs pa 'dus pa/ de bzhin gshegs pa thams cad kyi dgongs
pa 'dus pa'i rgyud,* Ng2.3.3.

[92]   *lang kar gshegs pa'i mdo, lankāvatrasūtra;* P775.

[93]   *rang mdangs.*

[94]   Paraphrasing Āryadeva's *Four Hundred Stanzas on the Yogic
Deeds of Bodhisattvas,* stanza 180 (VIII.5); sde dge 3846, 9a.7.
See Karen Lang, *Āryadeva's Catuḥṣataka: On the Bodhisattva's
Cultivation of Merit and Knowledge,* Indiske Studier 7 (Copenha-
gen: Akademisk Forlag, 1986), 81; and *Yogic Deeds of Bodhisatt-
vas: Gyel-tsap on Āryadeva's Four Hundred,* commentary by Geshe
Sonam Rinchen, translated and edited by Ruth Sonam (Ithaca,
N.Y.: Snow Lion Publications, 1994), 188. The entire stanza is:

> Those of little merit would not even generate
> Mere doubt about this doctrine.
> Even through merely coming to doubt it
> Cyclic existence is torn to tatters.

[95]   *ka dag*

[96]   *lhun grub.*

[97]   *dbyings.*

[98]   *stong pa nyid.*

[99]   *rang mdangs.*

[100] *gnyug ma'i sems.*

[101] *gnyug ma'i yid.*

[102] *rang bzhin 'od gsal ba'i sems.*

[103] *sems kyi rdo rje.*

[104] *mkha' khyab mkha' yi rdo rje can.*

[105] *rang bzhin bab kyi chos nyid.*

[106] *gzung 'dzin.*

[107] *chos nyid kyi rigs/rig pa.*

[108] *rang mtshan pa.*

[109] *rgyud kyi rgyal po rdo rje sems dpa' sgyu 'phrul dra ba/ rdo rje sems dpa'i sgyu 'phrul dra ba gsang ba thams cad kyi me long zhes bya ba'i rgyud,* THDL Ng3.1.2.1.2.

[110] *spros bral don gsal chen po'i rgyud,* THDL Ng1.5.1.

[111] *kun gzhi rnam par shes pa, ālayavijñāna.*

[112] *gsal rig.*

[113] *stong gsal.*

[114] *chos nyid gnyug ma'i sems.*

[115] *rdzogs chen nges don 'dus pa'i rgyud/ lta ba thams cad kyi snying po rin po che rnam par bkod pa,* THDL Ng1.5.17.

[116] *zang thal.*

[117] *rang byung ye shes.*

[118] *'od gsal ba'i ye shes.*

[119] XIII.19cd; Sanskrit in Sylvain Lévi, *Mahāyāna-Sūtrālaṃkāra, exposé de la doctrine du Grand Véhicule selon le Système Yogācāra,* tome 1 (Paris: Bibliothèque de l'École des Hautes Études, 1907), 88: *na dharmatācittamṛte 'nyacetasaḥ prabhāsvaratvaṃ prakṛtau vidhīyate //.*

[120] I.63ab.

[121] *rdzogs chen nges don 'dus pa'i rgyud/ lta ba thams cad kyi snying po rin po che rnam par bkod pa,* THDL Ng1.5.17.

[122] *kun tu bzang po ye shes klong gi rgyud rin chen gser gyi yang zhun/ rdzogs pa chen po nges don 'dus pa'i yang snying,* THDL Ng1.5.23.

[123] *rdzogs chen nam mkha' dang mnyam pa'i rgyud,* THDL Ng1.5.24.

[124] *rdzogs chen lta ba ye shes gting rdzogs kyi rgyud,* THDL Ng1.1.3.21.

[125] *rig pa rang shar chen po'i rgyud,* THDL Ng1.3.3.3.

[126] *chos, dharma;* this could also be translated as "practices."

[127] *rang grol.*

[128] *kun tu bzang po thugs kyi me long gi rgyud,* THDL Ng1.3.3.14.

[129] *rdzogs chen seng ge rtsal rdzogs kyi rgyud / seng ge rtsal rdzogs chen po'i rgyud,* THDL Ng1.3.3.8.

[130] *nor bu phra bkod/ nor bu phra bkod rang gi don thams cad gsal bar byed pa'i rgyud,* THDL Ng1.3.3.16.

[131] *klong chen rab 'byams rgyal po'i rgyud,* THDL Ng1.2.1.

[132] *rdzogs pa chen po rje btsan dam pa,* THDL Ng4.1.16.

[133] *kun byed rgyal po/ chos thams cad rdzogs pa chen po byang chub kyi sems kun byed rgyal po,* THDL Ng1.1.2.1.

[134] *padma dbang chen bde gshegs spyi dril gyi rgyud/ de bzhin gshegs pa thams cad kyi dgongs pa spyi dril gyi rgyud,* THDL Ng2.3.4.

[135] *sgyu 'phrul gsang ba snying po,* THDL Ng3.1.1.1.

[136] *sgyu 'phrul thal ba'i rgyud chen po,* THDL Ng3.1.2.1.4.

[137] *phyag rgya chen po, mahāmudrā.*

[138] *gsang ba 'dus pa;* P81, vol. 3.

[139] *kye rdo rje;* P10, vol. 1.

[140] *glang po rab 'bog gi rgyud,* THDL Ng3.1.3.3.5.

[141] *rdzogs pa chen po lta ba'i yang snying nam mkha' klong yangs kyi rgyud,* THDL Ng1.5.20.

[142] *ye shes gsang ba'i sgron ma rin po che man ngag gi rgyud,* THDL Ng1.2.7.

[143] *'jam dbyangs mkhyen brtse'i dbang po.*

[144] *rig 'dzin.*

[145] *dga' rab rdo rje.*

[146] *rnam rtog dang mtshan ma'i gzung 'dzin med pa.*

[147] *mtshan ma.*

[148] *shin tu spros med/ shin tu spros pa med pa de kho na nyid kyi man ngag ces bya ba* (*suniṣprapañcatattvopadeśa-nāma*); P2876.

[149] *srab mo'i 'od gsal.*

[150] *dga' rab rdo rje,*

[151] *rgyal ba rig 'dzin.*

[152] *mi pham 'jam dpal dgyes pa'i rdo rje.*

[153] *bstan gnyis dar rgyas gling.*

Index

Printed in the United States
by Bookmasters

Printed in the United States
By Bookmasters